The
Thoughtful Home

The Thoughtful Home

Dia Boyle

 Scepter

Published by Scepter Publishers, Inc.
info@scepterpublishers.org
www.scepterpublishers.org
800-322-8773
New York

Cover Image: Adobe Stock
Cover Art: DeLight Design
Text Design and Pagination: Studio Red Design

Paperback ISBN: 978-1-59417-537-4
eBook ISBN: 978-1-59417-538-1
Library of Congress Control Number: 2024944926

Printed in the United States of America

*In gratitude to Dolores
and Maria Dolores,
who made the homes that formed me.*

Contents

The Thoughtful Home

Flannery O'Connor tells the story of young Tarwater, an orphaned boy raised in a backwoods cabin by his mad, moonshine-making great uncle, who leaves his home and goes to the city for the first time. Looking around, he observes that unlike back home, "you have to do something particular here to make them look at you.... They ain't going to look at you just because you're here."[1]

This boy senses that what characterizes the home, even his eccentric and impoverished home, is that in it one can expect to be looked at, attended to, "just because you're here." He senses, perhaps, that a home is a place where one does not have to earn or demand or deserve attention, but where one is thought about and paid attention to precisely because he is at home.

Every human being has needs, fundamental and yet unique to the individual. The needs of a toddler are not the same as those of a teenager; the needs of an extrovert are not the same as those of an introvert;

---

1. Flannery O'Connor, *The Violent Bear It Away* in *Collected Works*. Literary Classics of the United States. (New York: Library of America, 1988), p. 347.

the needs of one old lady are not the same as those of her elderly neighbors. These needs must be thought about, they must be seen and understood, before they can be met. And these needs must be met, in order for the person to flourish. A man living on the street is homeless, and we can see with our own eyes that he is not flourishing. He is not living according to the dignity of his human nature. He does not live in a place where his needs are being attended to.

These needs are not limited to the material. There are many people, young and old, who have more than adequate food, clothing, and shelter, but do not live in a good home. They do not live in a place where their well-being is thought about, where they "look at you just because you're here." Such people, although not materially deprived, are also, in a real way, homeless. They, too, do not flourish, do not live in a way worthy of the dignity of their human nature.

We all need to be looked at, paid attention to, thought about. We all need to live in thoughtful homes. *Thoughtful* is a word with two layers of meaning. It means "marked by careful thought or consideration," as in a thoughtful essay. The opposite of this sense of *thoughtful* is "superficial." *Thoughtful* also means "showing consideration for the needs and well-being of others," as in a thoughtful gesture. The opposite sense here would be "thoughtless" or "impersonal." Both senses of *thoughtful* describe the good homes we need.

We would do well to consider the essentials of such a thoughtful home. How do we ensure that our families live in homes where their needs—material needs, but also emotional, intellectual, and spiritual needs—are observed, understood, and attended to? How do we make our own homes thoughtful homes?

Because our homes are ordinary, we take them for granted. Because we live in them, it is hard to see them objectively. Because they are so private and personal, our thoughts and feelings about them are complicated. It will serve us, especially those of us immersed in making and keeping a home, to give careful consideration to the home and to the needs of those who dwell within.

In the first part of this book, I suggest that because we no longer have a clear idea of what the home is and what it ought to be, we don't know for certain what we are trying to achieve in our work. It is this lack of certainty that underlies many of our worries and anxieties. In the second part, I explore the nature of the home: what it is, what it is for, and how it comes to be. I then consider, in the light of these explorations, what is required for a home to be, in fact, a good home. In the third part, I offer some time-honored means for making a good home in spite of our personal and cultural challenges. I conclude by considering the importance of the home beyond ourselves and our families.

Thinking about the home carries with it a special challenge. Our homes are not only intimately connected with our personal happiness, but with the happiness of our families. We love our families especially, and we are especially responsible for them. The ideas in *The Thoughtful Home*, therefore, touch not only on our happiness, but on our responsibilities: what we ought to do for the happiness of those who matter most to us. For this reason, these ideas carry with them a great potential for sadness, discouragement, guilt, and defensiveness, and we do not like to think about things which cause us pain.

Those of you who are beginners in the work of making a home are therefore at an advantage in thinking about the home. Your very lack of personal experience means that you are not yet set in your ways, not yet discouraged, not yet burdened by failure. This book is very much for the hopeful among us; I hope it equips you to plan and act with confidence, inspiring you to think deeply, work hard, and make the sacrifices necessary to achieve your goals.

These ideas, however, are not just for new recruits. They are for all of us. We all need to live in thoughtful homes. This book is, therefore, also for those already engaged in the battle, overwhelmed perhaps by a houseful of young children and the demands of a career. I hope it will help you to see clearly in the fog of war, to identify the most important things, and fight for them with all your strength. *The Thoughtful Home* is also for battle-weary and wounded veterans, those among us whose lives contain what seem like sad, hard failures in marriage and family life, some hidden but others that the whole world can see and judge. It is for those of you who feel that you are doing your best and yet things aren't going so well. It is for those who think, filled with regret, "If only I had known this earlier, or tried harder..."

Rather than causing guilt or pain, I pray these words will heal and nurture the bruised reed and rekindle the smoldering wick. It is important to remember that we can always change, and we can always change for the better. Any successes will be triumphs in a most noble cause.

PART I

Foundations

Chapter 1
Does Home Matter?

Almost all of us who work at making and running a home have a sense of the importance of this endeavor. For some of us, this sense is explicit. We know from our own childhood experiences, from reading various studies and articles, from observing social changes and cultural realities, how closely the nature and quality of the circumstances of the home are correlated with outcomes in marital happiness, school performance, and mental and physical health. We are burdened by this responsibility, worrying about the damage we might be doing, unintentionally, as a result of our ignorance, incompetence, lack of character, or even our sinfulness and hurts.

Many of us, however, may not have given much thought to the home, and only experience this sense of its importance in the form of anxiety and worry. We may tell ourselves that our concern and attention about the state of our homes is for those who don't have enough to think about, that children are resilient, and that on one's deathbed no one cares whether the dishes are done. Or we may think that our spouse will have to be the one to manage this aspect of our family life, since we are clearly too busy to worry about it. But still, we are anxious and irritated. We don't like living in a home that is out of control, that doesn't have order and routine. We are uncomfortable with how much the life in our home seems to be dominated by screens and the digital world. We can't help wondering about how this is affecting those we love: our spouses and our children. We hesitate to invite people over because we are not confident about our homes, and the way we live in them. We are afraid of what others will think, of what others will see, about our lives. We don't know what is wrong, or even whether something is wrong. We tell ourselves that we are silly to feel this way, but still, we aren't at peace.

No one enjoys anxiety. No one likes worrying. No one likes feeling incompetent or out of control. And so, we seek solutions. The first place we look, modern consumers that we are, is to what we can purchase. We figure we must be lacking something: something new, something better, something different. Perhaps what we need is a new appliance which would help us to do our work more efficiently. Maybe what we need is a better planner to help us make better use of our time, or a better app for communicating with others in the family and dividing the labor of daily chores. Maybe a different exercise regimen, so that we have more energy and self-confidence, or a new closet organizing system, or a menu planning app for our phone. Perhaps hiring help from the outside is the solution: more childcare, a meal delivery service, or a house cleaner. Maybe the answer is to enroll in a class or a tutorial to acquire a new skill. We adore novelty because novelty means change, and change invites us to hope.

The world is more than eager to help! Our friends tell us what a game changer their new purchase, their new app, their new online class is proving to be. Podcasts and websites which offer needed advice are also monetized, and once we research some new product—even before we decide to submit our order—we are flooded with suggestions of many more things we might need. Advertising finds its way into every nook and cranny of our lives, saturating our entertainment and following us, by means of our phones, into our most private spaces.

Unfortunately, new acquisitions don't eliminate or even reduce our anxiety. In fact, more often than not, they exacerbate it. The products, systems, and strategies which promise to improve our homes and simplify our lives instead raise our standards and expectations. More than a century ago, the washing machine eliminated the heavy work of the laundry tub but dramatically raised the cultural standard for what it means for clothes to be clean. What was once a weekly labor is now, for many of us, a daily and never-ending chore. What once required a laundry tub and washboard now requires its own room, which must itself be kept clean and up to date. Our smartphones have made it possible to know where our loved ones are at every moment, but don't seem to have drawn us any closer. Our organizational app helps us to be systematic in our cleaning, but also provides a never-ending to-do list of things we didn't know needed doing. We do not want to return to the laundry tub or the landline, but our front-loading high efficiency washing machine is not the answer to our anxiety.

My sixth-grade teacher told my parents that I needed an "attitude adjustment." If we don't need something more or better, perhaps we need to change the way we think about our homes and the work of making and keeping our homes. If we adjust our attitude, perhaps we will find peace and contentment.

Perhaps, too, we need to lighten up. This is often the advice of our friends and our fellow parents and the countless voices on social media who seem to understand our situation so well. They tell us to stop worrying so much, that "the kids are all right," and that there are far more things to be concerned about as a family than sparkling windows and homemade cookies. Our spouse or other family members may tell us that it is unrealistic to have family dinner every day, and not worth the effort to train our children to do chores. They assure us that those who claim to have met such expectations are either lying or miserable.

These well-meaning advisors encourage us to lower our standards and find more time for ourselves. Though welcome in small doses to keep our perfectionism in check, this kind of advice, if taken too seriously, belittles our homes and the work required to make and keep them. We know that when we lower our standards, our children still get hungry and our houses still get dirty, and all the self-care in the world does not take away the anxiety and irritation that flow from this state of affairs.

Maybe what we need is to get serious. If we would adopt a more serious attitude and accept the importance and nobility of the work of the home, our doubts and anxieties would fall away. We would be able to soldier on proudly, working more efficiently, getting home from work earlier, gladly giving up coffee breaks and paid vacations for the privilege of serving our families and, in them, our communities and our faith. This message often comes from more traditional sources. This advice is inspiring, and we make earnest resolutions to work harder and with more order. But again and again our resolutions don't stick. We find that being convinced of the great importance of our work but unable to carry it out competently does not alleviate our anxiety but increases it.

Finally, disappointed by our new acquisitions and disheartened by our attempts to change our attitude, we become aware of a siren song. This song, sometimes delivered in sophisticated therapeutic language and sometimes in the form of funny slogans stitched on dish towels, entices us to escape. If we cannot solve our anxieties, surely, we can escape them.

This is not a new song. In a past era, this escape, for women, might have taken the form of gossiping over the back fence or watching soap operas. For men, it might have taken the form of staying later than necessary at work or retreating behind the newspaper. Today we are enticed to escape into the endless amusements of our screens, paired with Trader Joes' dark chocolate-covered almonds and a little too much wine. And yet, most of us know from experience that such escapes, however welcome in the moment, do not permanently remove the least bit of our anxiety. When we return from our escapades, the dishes have piled up in the sink, the children have not finished their homework, and we feel a headache coming on.

So, what are we to do? How can we address the anxiety we all seem to feel about our home? We could probably all use some new products, life hacks, and attitude adjustments. We might all benefit from a little rest and recreation. But in the end, could it be that our anxiety comes not from what we lack or how we think, but from the fact that we don't know what we are trying to achieve? Is it possible that our anxiety comes from not knowing where we are going?

If I am anxious about an upcoming car trip, my spouse might try to help by showing me how to pack more efficiently or checking the air pressure in my tires. My mother might suggest that I postpone the trip until I feel better, and my pastor might advise me to ignore my feelings and press on. My best friend might give me audiobooks and travel snacks to help distract me from my anxiety. None of this well-meaning help will be useful, however, if I don't know where I am going and why. What might be good advice for a trip to the grocery store might be terrible advice for a cross-country drive to visit my dying grandmother. Until I know my destination and the purpose of my trip, their help and advice will only confuse me. Following it will increase rather than allay my anxiety.

Isn't this the reason that we find ourselves uncertain and anxious about the work of making and running a home? We all grew up in a home, we live in a home, and so we take it for granted that we know what a home is and what a home should be. We know what we mean by *homework*, *homestyle*, *homesick*, *hometown*, and *homeschool*. Certainly, we must know what we mean by *home*.

And yet, do we? Do we really know what a home is?

More importantly, do we know *why* a home is?

Do we know what the purpose of the home is, what a home is for?

Until we know the answers to these questions, we cannot know whether a product, a practice, a system, or an attitude is going to be helpful or harmful in our work. Until we are clear about what we are doing, we cannot have confidence in our choices and actions. For such clarity we need to consider these questions carefully and thoughtfully. Until we know the answers to these questions, our anxieties will continue to plague us.

Let us ask, then, in a thoughtful way, what a home is and what a home is for.

Chapter 2
Is It Practical to Be Thoughtful?

Have you ever noticed that in almost every kitchen pictured in a movie or on television, there is a bowl of fresh fruit on the counter? Fruit is pretty and colorful and we associate it with clean living. These ubiquitous images work on our subconscious. We turn off the movie, go into our own kitchens, and get a feeling that something is missing. So, we pull the fruit out of the refrigerator and pile it in a bowl. Of course, our fruit isn't as flawless as movie fruit, because it is real. The colors of the fruit don't really go with the color scheme of our kitchen. We don't have quite enough fruit to fill the bowl properly, because we didn't buy fruit for the purpose of decorating our kitchen but rather for feeding our family. Our counter space is limited, and we find ourselves moving the fruit bowl around to make space for cooking and washing up. After a few days, we start to notice fruit flies and the odor of overripe bananas. If we are confident, we laugh and realize that maybe a fruit bowl on the counter is not a very practical idea, at least not right now. But if we aren't so confident, we might feel like we have failed. We might feel like we can't even do something as simple as keeping a bowl of fruit on our counter.

We are not going to talk about whether there should be a bowl of fresh fruit on your kitchen counter, however. The first task of this book is to try to understand what a home is or, more precisely, what a home *ought* to be. We might determine, for example, that a home ought to be clean and orderly, or that meals in the home ought to be nutritious and appealing. This book will not give you a cleaning schedule or cleaning methods. Neither will this book discuss meal planning or provide culinary instruction.

"Wait!" you say. You might be thinking that this is not the book you were looking for. You might also be thinking that you don't even have time to read this book. "Look," you say, "I'm swamped and harried and overwhelmed, and as has been already pointed out, I am anxious! What a home *ought* to be? That sounds like philosophy! I don't have time for philosophy. I don't have time for ideals. Give me rules, give me a system! Give me a selection of home-related podcasts which I can listen to in the name of getting organized! Just tell me what to do and I will do it! Tell me where to put my fruit! Be practical, for goodness sake!"

Please believe me when I tell you that I understand your impatience. Yet it is practical, deeply practical, to think about the home not only as a problem to be bemoaned, solved, or eliminated, but as an idea to be thoughtfully considered. We must know what a home ought to be before we can know whether any particular task, approach, system, or app is important, essential, helpful, or a waste of energy. Regular family meals? Fresh fruit on the kitchen counter? Laundering the mattress pads semiannually? Sleep training? Only when I know what a home is—what it ought to be—can I determine whether a given product or practice or system belongs in my home, contributes to the good of my home, or is harmful to my home.

What a home is and what it ought to be *are* philosophical questions, and many of us hold a strong negative bias toward philosophical inquiry. Our American culture is famously pragmatic; we want to act boldly and accomplish great things, not think about them. Our modern culture is deeply influenced by relativism and individualism, and we are suspicious of "ought" statements. We do not like anyone telling us what we ought to do. Our personal history comes into play here, too, if personal experience of a bad college philosophy class led us to think of philosophy as frustrating, confusing, or pointless.

What is more, we are drawn to the particular, not the general. We are delighted by this flower, not the concept of flower. We love this person, not humanity. We are attracted to this or that home—Laura Ingalls Wilder's little house on the prairie, Downton Abbey, our childhood home—and not to the idea of the home. What is causing us anxiety is not an abstract idea or a philosophical question, but our particular, messy, chaotic, and overwhelming homes.

It will serve us well to try to overcome our dislike and distrust of philosophy, at least in this consideration of the home. Perhaps it will make us more comfortable to call this question "fundamental" rather than philosophical. After all, we don't mind signing our sons and daughters up for a workshop on the fundamentals of baseball. Calling it fundamental might help us understand that asking the philosophical question "What ought a home to be?" is a deeply practical exercise.

After all, the "fundament" or foundation of a building is of immense practical importance. No one falls in love with a house for the sake of its strong foundation, and when we are falling in love with a house, we are impatient with the inspection process. Yet if we learn that the foundation of the house we love is cracked or deteriorating, we realize that it is not practical to buy this house. And if we do buy it, choosing beauty or price or its dream kitchen over a sound foundation, we will sooner or later come to regret our choice or pay a great deal to repair it. Asking "What is a home?" is not a waste of time, but a fundamental question. Upon the answer to this question we can build a solid, stable, and enduring structure, constructed of a whole set of our own personal decisions, routines, materials, and attitudes.

In books and websites about the home, it is common that an accomplished and experienced authority describes what she does and how she does it. She shows you beautiful (albeit staged) photos of her outcomes. She shows you where she puts her fruit. She invites you to follow her example. What she shows can spark ideas about what might work in your own home, can inspire and encourage you to try a little harder, to bring more beauty, order, color, or discipline into your home.

Yet her home and her circumstances are not the same as yours; they are often vastly different. She has a small family, and yours is large, or vice versa. Her children seem studious, and yours are rambunctious. She is wealthy and you are in financially strained circumstances. How can her methods help you in any practical way? The peace and quiet of her home, the sophisticated menus, the intellectual level of the dinner-table conversations might make you feel like a failure because your home is full of noise and macaroni and potty humor. Copying her specific choices and methods might seem practical but will easily lead you to consumerism. You start to crave and covet that immaculate pantry, those sweet candles, that sunny southern exposure, those clearly contented and well-educated children gathered around that live-edge kitchen table. Comparing her home to yours will easily lead to despair.

Our individual homes are unique, almost overwhelmingly so. This is because each home is determined by the talents, tastes, training, and personality of the homemaker; by the number, ages, temperaments, and special needs of those who live there; by the economic resources of the family; by the neighborhood and culture in which the home is made; by a list of variables which is virtually infinite. For this reason, it will not be helpful for me to tell you how I run my own home, even though I love my home and even though you might be curious about it. When asked for advice, I am tempted to say, "This is what I do, and this is how I do it." If you ask me what you should serve for dinner, it is easy for me to give you my meal plan for the week, with recipes and a shopping list. But this will only be helpful if your family is like mine, if your cooking ability is like mine, if your food budget is like mine. Looking at my meal plan might give you new ideas and inspire you. But it might also depress you or make you anxious. "Really?" you say, despairing. "You do *all* this?" Or "Really?" you say, disappointed. "*This* is all you do?"

If we want to know where we are going, it is not helpful to borrow someone else's itinerary. Only when we find out what our destination is, can we determine our own itinerary. We get good ideas and inspiration from other people's homes, our friends' homes, the ones described in novels and staged in the movies, the ones pictured on Houzz and Pinterest. But we also get false needs, false hopes, and more and more anxiety. In the following chapters we are not going to talk about any particular and specific home, except by way of example. Instead, we will explore what a home ought to be, what any home and every home ought to be.

By asking and answering this question, we do not aim to identify the "perfect" home, for no home is perfect. In considering what a home is and ought to be, we will develop a sort of building code for our homes. A building code for a house doesn't prescribe the square footage of a house, the number of rooms, or the color of the paint, but it offers the minimum design and construction requirements to ensure a safe and resilient structure.

Our version of a building code will not prescribe a particular meal plan, daily schedule, or method of doing laundry. What we will develop by exploring the nature and purpose of the home is an understanding of what must be present in any and every home for it to fulfill the purpose of a home, in order for it to be a good home.

With this building code for the home, you will be able to decide whether a bowl of fresh fruit belongs on your own kitchen counter. You will be able to judge whether this detail contributes to the good of your home, is unnecessary, or even detrimental to it. If you decide such a practice would be useful and helpful, you will be able to come up with a strategy for accomplishing it, while taking into consideration your individual resources and challenges. Your anxiety will be exchanged for confidence. Knowing what a home is and what it ought to be will give you confidence to make all the decisions concerning your home, including those which you do not or cannot yet foresee. What could be more practical than that?

PART II

The Home

Chapter 3
What Is a Home?

We turn, then, to the question of what a home is. This might seem like an easy question to answer. In fact, it might seem like a question that should not have to be asked. It isn't like asking what TikTok is, or what breadfruit is, or what the French Revolution is. After all, almost everyone has had the experience of living in a home, and many of those reading this book have been deeply involved, in one way or another, in making and maintaining a home.

My mother's trusty college dictionary, passed down to me and now sitting on the shelf above my desk, defines *home* as "one's dwelling place, the abode of one's family."[2] This is correct, as far as it goes, for certainly our idea of home includes place and material structure (abode). When I say that I am going home, this is not a mental exercise but something which requires a car or a bicycle or my own two feet. When I invite you to my

---

2. *Webster's New Collegiate Dictionary*, 2nd ed., s.v. "home."

home, you need to know the street address. This might seem terribly obvious. But in a culture of virtual reality, of Instagram and Pinterest, we can sometimes forget that the home is not just a collection of beautifully edited images and ideas but is made of bricks and mortar (or mud and thatch). This material structure shelters those within from the elements and provides a place to store, prepare, and enjoy food, to sleep comfortably and safely, to wash, change, and care for our bodily needs.

This material structure provides not only shelter, but a space for common life, a space in which the family can gather to be together, to talk, work, study, play, laugh, and cry together. This private space, made private by means of the material structure which separates it from public life, makes family life possible. A material structure allows for the committed and loving human contact which is necessary for emotional development and cultural, intellectual, and spiritual formation.

This material structure admits of vast variety. A home can be made in a penthouse apartment on Fifth Avenue in New York, in a sod shanty on the prairie, or in a three-bedroom ranch style house in the suburbs. What these structures have in common is that they provide space and protection for human life and family life.

Clearly, however, the home is something more than this material structure. When a realtor says she has three homes to show us, we know that this is realtor jargon. She is going to show us three houses, three material structures, preferably empty ones. One can't buy a home; one can only buy a house. When we say that someone comes from a "broken home," we are not talking about his house's state of repair. When we observe that someone comes from a "good home," we don't need to know the real estate prices in his neighborhood. The way we use these words recognizes that a home is different from—and more than—a house.

The home, then, is not only the material structure we call a house (or apartment, castle, or shanty), but also the life that goes on within that structure. It is the nature of that life, far more than the nature of the material structure, which makes it a good or a broken home. Due to excruciating family circumstances, a friend spent several years of his childhood living with his family in a rat-infested motel room in a Mexican border town. This man remembers with gratitude the home and family life that his parents, with sacrifice, courage, ingenuity, and hope, created there. Likewise, it is easy to imagine beautiful houses, well stocked with all sorts of consumer goods, which do not feel or function like homes. Those who live there fend for themselves, eating what they find in the well stocked refrigerator, amusing themselves with electronics in their comfortable and isolating bedrooms. These houses do not feel like homes, precisely because there is no common life within them.

Will it work, then, to define the home as "a material structure and the life that goes on within it"? This definition is still too broad, for it describes not only the home, but many other places where we might live for a time: hospitals, army barracks, college dormitories, and all the other places which, sooner or later, we long to leave in order to "go home." More important, especially for our purposes, this definition of the home does not satisfy those of us who care about the home. This definition does nothing to alleviate our anxieties, inform our decisions, or order our work. We sense that "home" is more specific still, that it names a particular kind of structure containing a particular kind of life. We must dig deeper to find out what we want to know: a concept of home which will tell us what we are aiming for, where we are going, what our goal is. The dictionary definition will not do. We must *study* what a home is.

When we want to study something, not just name it, we look at it carefully, noting its different parts and its function. We look at as many instances of that thing as we can find, and try to determine what all these individual things have in common: What parts do they all have? What functions do they all share?

If we want to know what a knife is, we could go to our kitchen and gather up all the different things we call *knife*. We could study a chef's knife, a butter knife, a bread knife, a steak knife, and a paring knife. We would note that these knives aren't interchangeable. We use one for one job and a different one for a different job. Why, we ask, do we name them all *knife*? We recognize that all these different knives have the same parts: a blade and a handle. We realize that all these knives have a similar purpose: they are for cutting. We can think of other things that are for cutting: scissors and razor blades and Weedwackers. But we don't call all cutting instruments *knives*, only those with a single blade and a handle. Continuing our study, we realize that different knives are designed to cut different things, and this purpose determines their design: a chef's knife is for cutting vegetables, a butter knife for butter, a bread knife for bread. But they all share the same parts and function: they have a blade which is sharp and strong enough to cut what they are designed to cut, and they have a handle suited to the person doing the cutting.

When we want to study the home in the same way, we encounter a problem. Knives are simple, but homes are complicated. We are not able to study many instances of homes, certainly not in the deep and intimate way that such a complex reality requires. Homes have myriad parts, and the parts are not only four walls and a roof, but the life that happens within. It is hard to gather and study many instances of homes because, unlike the knives in our drawers, homes are private. We can't know them unless we are invited in, and even when this happens, we can only know what is shown to us in that moment. We are only very rarely free to examine closely a home that is not our own, free to study all its parts. The ordinary parts of a home, such as the everyday meals, bedtime routines, and general cleanliness, are not seen by the guest, for the home doesn't follow its ordinary routines when guests are present. This privacy is a fundamental function of the home, protecting intimate family life from public view for the sake of that family life. If we could be present in others' homes as neutral and unseen observers, we would have a chance of studying those homes in depth, but the idea of having, or being such an observer is unsettling to say the least.

The homes we actually can study, because they are (or were) our own homes or "like a second home" to us, we cannot study with objectivity. My childhood home, for good or ill, shaped me, and yours shaped you. It shaped the way I think about what a home is and ought to be. It shaped my habits and routines, as well as my attitude toward the work of making a home. Some of us came from good homes, and some of us did not. And because both the good ones and the not-so-good are the only homes we have known, we are often not aware of what was missing in them, what could have been done better, and what was done right. Because we have only known a very few homes intimately and deeply, we are not always aware that our thoughts and assumptions about what a home is supposed to be are not universal. We may still not really know that everyone doesn't eat dinner together every night (or that anyone *does* do so!), or that every mother doesn't have a hot temper, or that bathrooms are not always clean. We probably have an idea in our minds of what a home should be like either because it is the way our home was, or the way we wish our home had been. Depending on our own personalities, we might assume that all other homes fall short in the same ways that ours falls short, assuring us that such shortcomings are unavoidable. Or, we might assume that all other homes are ideal and only ours falls short, making us embarrassed and anxious.

Literature allows us to experience other homes remarkably intimately. I feel almost as knowledgeable about Laura Ingalls' childhood home as I am about my own. Literature allows us to experience ways of living and thinking which our own personal experience could never provide. Yet as powerful and memorable as these depictions are, these literary homes are usually from different eras and do not reflect our own realities. Their depictions are colored by sentiment, nostalgia, and the authors' purposes.

In other eras, we might have had a much better sense of what was happening in other homes even without being invited in, because of a powerful and shared culture of the home. There was a time in our own culture when almost everyone did the laundry on the same day, and it was hung to dry outside, so everyone could see how white the whites were and how often the sheets and towels were changed. Children from many families played together in the neighborhood, and they could know, from when their playmates were called in for dinner or to do chores, the routines and schedules of other homes. There were fewer choices in the grocery stores and no recipes on the Internet, and so the neighbors' menus were likely to be similar to our own. Ethnic communities were also stronger and immigration meant living in closer proximity to others who shared both culture and native language. Now, our standard of living makes it possible for laundry to be done any day, and for our choices of consumer goods to be unlimited by our geography. Urban homogenization has vastly limited distinctive local goods. We are unlikely to know, unless we ask, when or whether our friends and neighbors do their laundry or eat dinner together as a family.

All is not lost, however, in our desire to study the home more deeply. What we cannot learn from wide experience, we can learn from authority. We do not have to experience the flora and fauna of the jungle.

We can read about the trees and apes and insects in the rainforest, or listen to a podcast on its ecosystem, or learn from friends and colleagues who have traveled there. Of course, the reliability of what we learn from authority depends on the reliability of the authority. What we learn from Kipling's *Just So Stories* or our neighbor's vacation photos may be at odds with what we learn from National Geographic videos or the *Ecology of the Equatorial Rainforest* textbook. Still, we are able to study the rainforest without experiencing it for ourselves.

Are there authorities who can help us in studying the home? Many decades ago, I was instructed in how to make and keep a home by my mother, who learned from her mother. Her maternal authority was reinforced or corrected by the home economics class that I, along with every girl in my public school, was required to take. The younger you are, however, the less likely your mother would have seen this work as something to be transmitted to the next generation for the sake of family survival and well-being. It may have been that we disregarded our mother's wisdom and considered it out-of-date or obsolete. Your mother may not have been able to be an authority even if she wanted to be. She may not have known what to teach or have been able to find the time to pass on her wisdom. Your mother may have been in the same state of ignorance and anxiety as you now find yourself. And while "home ec" may still exist in corners of our culture, it is no longer a strong enough institution to form or even influence a shared culture of the home.

Our present culture's most powerful authority on what homes should be are the images we view on the screens which fill our lives—images and depictions of homes in advertising, social media, television, and movies. They are produced and edited to be powerful and seductive, and they form our imaginations. We look at Pinterest and HGTV, and think we know how everyone else is designing their homes. We watch movies and television shows, and think we are viewing modern family life. We follow Instagram and listen to podcasts from those we admire, and assume we are seeing what their homes are really like. From these sources we form images of what a home ought to look like and how it ought to function. It is these images which often drive us into debt, anxiety, or despair.

And yet we cannot trust that these images, which so powerfully shape our imaginations, correspond to reality. We cannot trust them because the purpose of these "authorities" is not to help us study and understand reality, but to sell us products, attract advertisers, and increase followers. Truth is not the goal; product sales and web clicks are. If we relied on these images, we would think that every kitchen has a large bowl of perfect fruit on an impeccable counter, that paint is always flawless, and that children—if there are any—are always smiling.

Unable to rely on experience or authority, our study of the home must take a different approach. If I am poking around in a thrift shop and find a gadget I've never seen before, I might go up to the proprietor and ask, "What is this for?" When he tells me that it is for removing the pits from cherries, I am immediately enlightened. "Aha! It is a cherry pitter! Now I see!" I don't need to see and study five different instances of cherry pitting tools. I just needed to learn the purpose of the gadget I was wondering about. If we cannot study many individual homes, if we cannot learn from trustworthy authorities, we must study in a different way. We must study the *purpose* of the home, and we must ask what a home is for.

Chapter 4
What Is a Home For?

Humans, it seems, require a home. Every culture throughout human history has erected shelters to which individuals or, most often, families, return in the evening to eat and sleep and be together. Those who do not have a home—an infant raised in an institution, refugees and migrants on the move or in temporary camps, the homeless in American cities—are understood to be seriously disadvantaged. Not only is their physical health and even survival threatened, but their mental and emotional health are damaged. If the "happy vagabond" is happy, it is only because he has some sort of home. He either carries his home with him, in a nomad's tent or an Airstream, or he has a "home base" to which he can return.

Why do we have homes? Why, in spite of striking differences in philosophies, religions, climate, geography, wealth, technological progress, and human development, is it a demonstrable fact that human beings make and keep homes? It seems that the home, a common and universal human reality, must be common precisely because it solves a universal human problem, meets a universal human need, in an unparalleled way.

The home not only meets a universal human need, but it is uniquely human. Wild animals do not have homes. Birds have nests, but birds do not live in nests. They live in the woods, on the prairie, in the Everglades: they live in their habitats. A bird's nest is only a structure used for the purpose of incubating eggs and containing baby birds until they are able to fly. Nests are abandoned once the fledglings leave the nest. A bird's nest is more akin to our baby equipment than our home. When our children "leave the nest," we might give away their cribs and high chairs, but we don't abandon our homes. Under normal circumstances we live in a home not only when helpless and dependent, but throughout our entire lives. Why is this? Why do we need what animals do not seem to need: a secure place to call home?

Human beings need a home in order to be human.

Not, of course, to be "of the human species." A *homo sapiens* is a *homo sapiens* and can no more escape this chromosomal destiny than a crow can become a cat. But there is a difference here. A crow cannot be anything but a perfect crow. We say that someone is "free as a bird," but this is only poetry. Animals are not free; they do not choose. A crow can't decide to be a vegetarian, or move to Tahiti, or be a better crow. Animals pursue their prey and care for their young, but these are not choices. They act from instinct and cannot choose otherwise. Their instincts give them everything they need to flourish, so long as they are in their proper habitat. If they do not flourish, it is not because of their bad choices, but because of the deterioration of their habitat or their health. There are no truly bad crows, only unsuccessful ones.

But there are truly bad human beings. Because we have free will, we can choose to act inhumanely. We can do things, say things, believe things, that are not in accord with our human nature. Human flourishing is not simply a matter of survival and successful reproduction for the continuation of the species. Human flourishing is something much greater, something that instinct and habitat are not adequate to achieve on their own. Unlike animals, we have both free will and the power of reason, and so we can choose to act against our instincts or to transcend our instincts. Freed from our instincts, we have the terrible freedom to act like something other than a human. We can choose to act like a beast, or a monster—or an angel. Human beings need homes, and animals do not, for the simple and profound reason that *human beings are free.* Because we choose freely, we must be taught to choose well.

Our needs go beyond material survival. We have emotional, psychological, intellectual, and spiritual needs. We must be fed and sheltered, and later taught to find food and shelter—to hunt and build a cabin, to shop for groceries and apply for a mortgage—but we also must be taught to talk, to question, to ponder and make an argument. We must be guided to think about more than our bellies, and to appreciate that the world merits our attention, study, and wonder. We must also be taught that we matter, that our choices and words and actions have consequences. We must be helped to realize that others depend on us and should be able to trust and count on us. We must be encouraged and trained to think of others, to be patient, to share, to be loyal, to do our duty, to love. All of these come, not from within ourselves, nor from our instincts and biology. They come from our mothers, our fathers, our families, our schools and communities and churches, all of whom care for us and take care of us. To flourish as human beings, we must be cared for.

From our first moments on this earth, we have been cared for in a place where we were not only fed and clothed and bathed, but were listened to, paid attention to, corrected, guided, and challenged. This care happens, first and foremost, in the home. The home is the universal human solution to the universal human need for care. Human beings need to be cared for, and the home is where this happens. The care that allows us not only to survive but to flourish is ordinarily provided within and by means of the home; this is what a home is for. A child who grows up in a prosperous home but is not paid attention to, cared for, corrected, and inspired is deeply deprived. Infants raised in Soviet-era orphanages were permanently impaired.

This care, importantly, is not needed only by the young. Human beings not only learn how to be human but must be maintained in their humanity. We need to live with others throughout our lives, not simply for the safety of numbers, but to flourish in our humanity. We can see for ourselves what happens when someone lives without attentive care. A homeless woman living on the street is not able to maintain herself as her human dignity demands. Solitary confinement is one of our most severe punishments. Pandemics have demonstrated what we already suspected: that isolation, which can come about in many ways, is not healthy for us. We need to be with others not only to benefit from cooperation, but to be asked "How are you feeling?" "Why are you doing that?" "What were you thinking?!" We need to be with others in order to be happy and whole. We need a home so that we can receive the care and attention we need in order to survive, to flourish, and to be maintained in our humanity.

But does this happen only in a home? What about those other residential institutions where we live and find care, such as army barracks, hospitals, and hotels? We do find care there, but our experience assures us that these are not homes. Soldiers live in barracks while they are training for war, and they must endure being far from home. Patients live in hospitals when they are sick or injured, and they long to be discharged so that they can return home. Sales personnel, consultants, and tourists live in hotels because they are traveling away from home.

Why do army barracks and hospitals not feel like home? Because in these places everyone is treated in the same way: the care given is not ordered to the unique needs of the individual, but to the common needs of the soldier, the infirm, the traveler. These institutional places are designed not to ensure human flourishing in general, but to serve the special and temporary needs of a specific category of human beings: the soldier's need for training, the patient's need for healing, the traveler's need for temporary lodging. These residences allow only very minimal freedom for the private and individual pursuits and needs of the residents, since such individualization would either undermine the mission of the institution or require too many resources.

Revealingly, we do use the word *home* in the names of certain types of residential institutions: a group home, a nursing home, a home for unwed mothers, a veteran's home. These institutions are not private homes, but they are created to provide for the general, not special, needs of those who are unable, for one reason or another, to live in their own homes. The nursing home, for example, strives to provide for the general human needs of the infirm elderly: not just meals and medical care, but company, intellectual stimulation, affection, privacy, and everything, to the extent possible, that they would once have found in their own homes.

The contrast between an army barrack and a veterans' home, between a hospital and a group home, supports the conclusion that the purpose of the home is to provide for the care of human beings *as human beings*. The home is designed to meet more than one particular need or mission of those who live there, as a nest is for a baby bird or barracks are for an army. The home meets the general needs of the whole person throughout his whole life. The home is the ordinary place where we find the care we need as human beings, a place ordered not only to our biological survival, but to our emotional, psychological, intellectual, and spiritual needs as human beings.

Clearly, and regrettably, not everyone has a home. Certainly not everyone has a good home in any meaningful sense of the word, a home which succeeds in carrying out this mission of caring for humanity. This truth is manifest in our schools, our prisons, and our emergency rooms. Those we call "the homeless" are deprived of a place to live, not merely a place to sleep. Far more people, many of whom are children, despite having plenty of food and clothing and shelter, do not live in places where they are being attended to and cared for. Although they might reside in beautiful houses, they too are effectively "homeless." Those who live without a good home do not flourish, because the home is the place where we find the care we need to become human, to remain human, and to flourish in our humanity.

Chapter 5
Who Is a Home For?

We bought our first home when we had one child and hopes for many more. We bought a large and shabby house with plenty of bedrooms and bathrooms so that our family could expand in comfort, and so that we could offer hospitality to friends and colleagues and extended family. We chose a neighborhood very close to the university where my husband taught so that students could visit easily and often.

As the years passed, our family did not grow as much as we had hoped, and our first child grew into an introverted adolescent. He disliked that our house was often full of "strangers," as he called them. To him, our home did not feel like a private place. Consequently, he took advantage of the size of our house to hide away in an attic room or a corner of the basement.

Although we would miss our guest quarters and our spacious dining room, we realized that the purpose of our home was the care of our family. We understood that our home should be organized primarily and fundamentally for the care of that family. So, we decided to move from

40

that house to a smaller house, closer to our children's schools and friends, and more suited to our budget. With fewer places to hide and fewer "strangers" to hide from, our son naturally returned to the mix of family life. Our circumstances, of course, are different from yours. Where we needed a smaller house, you might need a larger one. But our homes are the same in that they should be made for the sake of the family that lives within. Our homes share the same purpose of making the care of our families both possible and probable.

Our homes are for our families. Family, regardless of our politics and ideologies, is a group of people who are related to one another in a permanent way, by blood or by law. Most typically, a family is parents and their children, but the name of *family* may also be given to the childless couple, the grandmother raising her grandchildren, and to siblings Marilla and Matthew raising orphan Anne at Green Gables. A home can be made for those who do not form a family, such as a group of unrelated housemates or a person living alone, but these non-family arrangements will succeed as homes to the extent that they approximate the sort of life ordinarily found in a family home. What sort of life is that?

Robert Frost says a home is "something you somehow haven't to deserve."[3] Families are unlike other groups of people in that the members of the family belong to the group not because of what they do, but simply

---

3. Robert Frost, "The Death of the Hired Man" in *North of Boston*, 2nd ed. (New York: Henry Holt and Company, 1914), p. 20.

because of *what they are*: mother, father, daughter, son. The members belong to the family not because they choose to belong to it, not because they share the same beliefs or follow the same lifestyle as the others in it, and certainly not because they have earned or merited their place in it. They do not live in the home because they deserve to be there. They live there because they are family. Because they are family, they belong.

The care that is given in a home is given on this very basis: those who live there are cared for not because they have earned the care, but because they need the care in order to flourish as human persons. Thanks to the family bond, those who live there will be cared for, as human beings, in and by means of the home. I do not feed my children so that they will be strong enough to labor in my fields, as I might feed hired hands. I do not feed them in exchange for payment, as I might feed boarders. I feed my children because they are my children and, as such, their flourishing is my responsibility and my desire. We guide our children to behave respectfully not because it is more comfortable for us to live with respectful people (although this is true), but because it is our responsibility as their parents to help them become virtuous men and women.

This family care is important, obviously, for the very young, since they cannot earn or merit or pay for anything at all. But even independent adults need the security of belonging so that they are free to be who they are, not limited to being what is useful or desirable to someone. If I am hired for a job, it is because there is work to be done and I have the skills to accomplish that work. But when that work is no longer necessary, or I am no longer able to accomplish it, I will be let go. Likewise, I can leave that work if I no longer want to do what I was hired to do. The bond between employee and employer is temporary and conditional. Those who dwell in a home, however, are there because they are the mother, the father, the daughter, the son. These relationships are permanent and unconditional. Children grow up and leave their homes in order to make homes of their own. The homes they leave never cease to be their homes, however. They will always retain a claim of belonging.

The residents in a home do not have to earn their care, and neither do they have to request or demand their care. This is not to say, of course, that they cannot or should not request care. Obviously, this will happen: "Could you iron my shirt?" "It's our turn to bring juice boxes to T-ball today!" "Mommy, play with me, I'm bored!" However, the care in a home ought not to be fundamentally by demand. If you don't order room service in a hotel, no one will know or care that you are hungry. If you do order room service, no one will tell you that what you need is protein and fiber, not chips and a Mountain Dew. In contrast, the care that is given in the home and by means of the home is given because someone there is paying attention to those who live there. Someone is studying what each one needs, noticing what is missing in the give and take of the life within. "Something is up with Annie. I wonder what is really going on." This kind of care is essential for our babies, who are not able to articulate their needs. But it is also needed by those who are able to speak—by our young children who do not know what it is that they need, our teenagers who refuse to tell us what they need, and our spouses who do not want to burden us with what they need. The care needed for someone to flourish as a human being must be determined before it can be given, which means a home must be a place where one is paid attention to and thought about, just because you're there.

For this to be the case, the life which happens within the family home should be private. More than once I observed that, in the few seconds it took for my daughter to say goodbye to her classmates on the sidewalk and walk up the path to our front door, her face changed from a calm public face to a face full of emotion. Her tears, held back ever since the playground drama which had provoked them, were falling as she crossed the threshold into the privacy of her home. In her home, she did not have to worry about hiding her emotions in order to fit in or be accepted. She knew that she did not have to be well-liked in order to have a place. In her home, shielded from the public eye, she was able to be herself and show her disappointment, anger, or fear.

This need for privacy is one of the reasons that a home is a material structure. The home should be a place where, ordinarily, the family is able to control the access the world is given to what is within its walls. If we want our homes to help us pay attention to and determine the needs of our families, we should realize that some of the most important needs will only be revealed if home is a safe place to expose our vulnerabilities. We will only be willing to disclose our needs and our weaknesses, as well as our gifts and our strengths, when we are confident that they will not be used to manipulate, punish, or exploit us. We need a home that allows us the privacy to be with those who value us for who we are and, likewise, protects us from those who value us only because we are useful to them or who fail to value us at all.

Our homes should not be fortresses, because living in a fortress is not healthy for a family. Opening our homes in hospitality allows us to help and enjoy those outside of our family circle, our guests and friends and children's friends. But even more importantly, our ordered hospitality helps our own families. When our children see us with our guests, observing how we treat them and the small sacrifices we make for them, they learn about friendship. When they eavesdrop on our conversations, they learn about adult life. When they notice how others listen to and respect our opinions, their own esteem for us grows naturally. In the end, however, hospitality must remain secondary to the primary purpose of the home, which is the care of those who live there. Our family homes should be open to the world in hospitality, but not determined by the world.

We should not take for granted the privacy of the home, and therefore fail to value and protect it. In totalitarian states, the privacy of the home is recognized as an enemy of the state and therefore is diminished in many ways. The state designs family housing, decides who lives there, and encourages those who live there to report on the private behavior of family members. Nazi Germany, Soviet Russia, and more recently, North Korea, understood the obstacle the private home poses to the ideological control of their people. These extreme

examples remind us not to assume that every way of
life promoted by the culture is good, simply because
it is more efficient or less expensive. Just as we would
not lightly open our homes to government surveillance,
we should be thoughtful about what we expose to the
public eye of the private life of our homes and families.
We should be careful about how widely we open our
homes to the curious eyes of marketing firms, political
organizations, and social media. This is part of making
our homes places where our families can flourish in
human freedom, thanks to the security made possible
by the family bond.

The family home, along with being private, should
be permanent. The home should be permanent not in
the sense of unchanging, but in the sense of the Latin
root *permanens*: staying, abiding, remaining. We should
be able to count on the home (not necessarily the
house). Whether a family lives in a house passed down
through generations or seldom lives at one address
for longer than a year, the home itself should always
be there. When our aging parents are no longer able
to live in their own home, we are sad for their loss of
independence. But we also grieve the loss of the home
our parents had continued to make for us, long after we
left to make homes of our own. When we leave home,
to go to college or to the hospital or to prison, we
count on it remaining in our absence, "the green, green
grass of home." When temporarily away from home, we
naturally put together a makeshift home wherever we
find ourselves, a temporary extension of our permanent
home. In our campsite, we place the camp chairs around

the fire pit and arrange the sleeping bags in the tent so that everyone has a place. In a hospital room, we bring in family photos and flowers to make the space more homey. We seem to understand that it is good for our emotional health to remember that we have a home, one that remains.

Of course, nothing human is entirely stable, predictable, or able to be counted on, because every human being is free: we are sinners, and are damaged by the failings of others. Members of families do betray one another. Family life can be chaotic or dysfunctional. There are even times when, for the sake of the family, one member must leave the home. And every human being is mortal. Eventually, we all die. Nevertheless, because the relationships that form the family are permanent (I do not cease to be their daughter if my father leaves my mother), the home and the care offered there should remain. Unlike school or workplace, it is the home to which the bridge of return is never burned.

What does it mean that a home is for a family? It means that those who dwell there can be confident that they belong, comfortable enough to let their needs be known, and secure enough to take the risks required for human flourishing. That a home is for a family means that those who dwell there are free to discover in the deepest possible sense who they are, and to become who they are meant to be. There is a reason that we consider homelessness a crisis. Every person needs a family, and every family needs a home.

Chapter 6
Does a Home Just Happen?

In Gertrude Chandler's *The Boxcar Children* series, a quartet of runaway orphans finds shelter from a thunderstorm in an abandoned boxcar. The children lay claim to the boxcar and decide to live there. When they came across that boxcar on that stormy night, they did not find a home. They found a material structure that could shelter them from the elements. It is the children who transform the boxcar into a home, and that began with intention. The children understood that if they were to stay together as a family, they had to have a home, a place to live in which their needs could be met in a stable way. This new home didn't just happen; it had to be made.

The home is an instrument. To talk and think of the home as an instrument could feel cold, given the emotional reality of the homes we know and love. If we temporarily strip away the emotion, however, we can see more clearly the rational framework underlying the emotional reality. Conceptually, we can distinguish between the home and the family. A homeless mother, living with her children in a car or an emergency shelter, does not love her children any less than one who has a home. Her children almost always prefer to be with her on the street rather than separated from her in a foster home. She loves them and will do whatever she can to meet her children's needs. Yet in such difficult circumstances, meeting their needs and her own is simply not sustainable. The heroic effort required of her to ensure that her children merely eat and sleep in safety leaves her barely any capacity to listen to them, discipline them, and consider what they need in order to grow and flourish. What is more, in these unstable conditions, the children don't always have the freedom to show their feelings and their needs. They are reluctant to cause more trouble. This homeless mother desires a home for her family precisely because with it and in it she would be better able to care for those she loves. Her maternal love makes her want to care for them well, and a home is the instrument she needs in order to realize her maternal desire.

For an instrument to be effective, it must be designed, then crafted, and then used. A chef cannot chop with just any old thing, an umbrella or a ball of twine. He needs a knife, an instrument designed for chopping. The more complicated the purpose of an instrument is, the more complicated its design. The needs of our families are complicated because our families are composed of complicated human beings. Not only do they have material needs, but emotional, psychological, cultural, intellectual, and spiritual needs. Since each person and each family is unique, each home's design must be unique.

The design of an instrument is important, but it is also true that a chef cannot chop with the design of a knife, no matter how perfect that design might be. The knife must be crafted, its design must be realized, before the chef can start chopping. Likewise, homes which we have planned and designed must be brought into being and maintained in being. Our homes must be made and kept.

The instrument of the home, finally, must be put to use. Julia Child's kitchen, a carefully preserved marvel of design and workmanship on display in the Smithsonian Museum, is a fascinating historical artifact. It was once an instrument for the care of her family but is no longer. If a home is to be an effective instrument, it must be put to use caring for those who dwell there.

All of this takes creativity and intelligence, but also the physical labor, practical skills, persistence, time, and energy of the one who makes the home, that is, the *homemaker*. Our culture does not like to talk about homemakers and homemaking. It is a subject fraught with cultural and ideological controversies. Nevertheless, we cannot afford to be put off by terminology. Homes don't make themselves. They don't happen by chance; they don't happen in nature. Homes have to be made, which means that someone has to make them. The modern home is breaking down in many places and circumstances in large part because no one is available to do this needed work, to give this needed care.

The word *homemaker* carries cultural baggage and is associated in some modern minds with aprons, homeschooling, and a lack of ambition. But *homemaker*, freed from cultural associations, names the agents who are paying attention to the needs of the different family members, determining what each one needs, and organizing and arranging things to make sure that those needs are being met. *Homemaker* names those who have the intention of creating and running the home for the purpose of encouraging, supporting, and making possible human flourishing.

Homemakers, along with those who help, put the home to use as an instrument. Her job (or his, or theirs) is to assess the needs of her family, to plan and make her home, and to give her family, using the instrument of the home, the care that they need. Her family, in contrast, is not an instrument. Her family cannot be planned, designed, produced, or used, because it is composed of human beings who are not (humanly speaking) planned, designed, and produced, and who *must* not be used. By means of the home, the homemaker cares for her family.

This care is essential. We human beings can be given a version of our perfect habitat: a house with well-prepared foods offered regularly, a desk with excellent lighting for study, a comfortable and quiet place to sleep, plenty of opportunities for meaningful human contact.

Yet we have no assurance that we will exploit this perfect habitat in such a way that we will live a flourishing human life. If left to ourselves in this habitat, isn't it just as likely that we will eat Doritos, binge on Netflix, and fall asleep on the couch? Or stay at the office, or out at the bar, never even taking advantage of this habitat?

Because we need care. So much of the time, as human beings, we don't know what we need, we don't want what we need, we can't get what we need, and we won't ask for what we need. We can't rely solely on our instincts because we are free and rational, and our needs are far more complicated than a squirrel's. Experienced parents know that a little boy who is whining and complaining of being hungry may indeed be hungry. But it is just as likely that he is bored, or tired, or feeling ignored. A child doesn't know what he needs. Adults, too, don't always know what they need, and even when they do, they may not be willing to ask for it; they may not have the time to obtain it; they may not want to accept it. Unlike squirrels, human beings have other things on their minds than mere survival.

How simple it would be if we could order our homes online, counting on Amazon's algorithms to determine and supply the needs of our families. But in this world, each one of us is unique, with a unique and complicated, evolving and changing set of needs. What a small boy needs is different from what a middle aged woman needs, and among the needs of small boys there are vast differences. One boy needs eggs for breakfast and another needs oatmeal. One needs a firm hand and another needs cheerful encouragement. One needs a military academy and another needs to learn at home. One needs solitude and one needs a vigorous social life. Ask the mother of identical twins whether her twins' needs are identical, and she will assure you that even when nature and nurture seem to be identical, their needs are not. We are complicated creatures.

In his novel *Brave New World*, Aldous Huxley imagines a world in which those in power set themselves the goal of eliminating suffering by meeting every human need. The designers of this brave new world understand that human needs are too complicated and varied to be met by a central agency. So, they endeavor to simplify peoples' needs by engineering the human beings themselves. By means of breeding and psychological conditioning, the government attempts to minimize human individuality, and thereby standardize human needs to those that can be efficiently met. The family is eliminated, because the family fosters individuality and the resulting individual needs. This brave new world is horrifying and inhumane. Fortunately for all of us, this experiment is a figment of Huxley's remarkable imagination.

Each person is a unique individual; therefore, each person has unique and individual needs. The homes in which these individuals find care must be individually designed and made to correspond to their individual needs. Those needs are not self-evident, nor can they be predetermined. Our homes, if they are to be good and successful homes, must be designed and made by someone who is paying attention to and thinking about the needs of each individual member as well as the needs of the family as a whole.

Those of us who are involved in the care of the family, who are reading this book because we sense the importance of the home to those we love, know who we are and know what we are. We are the ones who are paying attention to and thinking about our families, who are trying hard to figure out what they need to thrive, and to find ways to meet those needs. We are the agents of the home, its designers, producers, and keepers. Woman or man, traditional or trailblazer, as uncomfortable as our society is with the term, we know that we are the homemakers.

We are also the ones who, in and by means of the home we make, provide needed care. We put the instrument of the home to use. Returning to the simple example of chef and knife, it is obvious that the chef can't chop without the knife, and even more obvious that the knife can't chop without the chef. If we had to choose, it would be better to have a chef without a knife, than a knife without a chef. Without a knife the chef can still improvise–tear the food, use scissors, stew it whole ,and pull it apart. But a knife without a chef is absolutely useless. Similarly, a home without a homemaker isn't even a home. It is just a house full of stuff, that "perfect habitat" we considered before. Someone must make and keep the home. Someone must give the care.

"Homemaker" is not a lifestyle or an ideological identity. There are cardiologists and professors and manicurists and politicians who are also homemakers. We are homemakers when we transform a campsite into a temporary home. We are homemakers when we bring bedding and a mini-fridge and a potted plant into a dorm room. We are all, in one way or another, in need of the care of a homemaker. And we are all, in one way or another, called upon to be homemakers. This is a part of the human condition, and it only makes sense to address this reality with energy, intelligence, and determination, as well as with thoughtful reflection.

Chapter 7
Why a "Thoughtful" Home?

In saying that the home is what we need to flourish in our humanity, we do not mean that those who come from an impoverished or broken home are in any way less human, or that those who are homeless cease to be human. Certainly, such persons are faced with a more difficult struggle to live in accord with their natural human dignity, that is, to flourish. At the same time, we recognize that in the world of humankind, there is little that cannot be overcome by grace, hard work, and a helping hand. The good home, however, is the ordinary path to human flourishing; in and by means of such a home, human flourishing happens in a natural and reliable way. Without such a home, there will be much that will need to be overcome.

Our homes, of course, must be more than an idea, more than a platitude like "Home is where the heart is." Our homes must be more than the beautiful photographs and romantic writing of our favorite lifestyle influencer.

Real homes are *made*, not purchased; they are not "consumer goods." The daily physical, emotional, and intellectual work of making and maintaining our homes is challenging, and taking on this challenging work is of key importance precisely because the good home is such an effective and indispensable instrument for the care of our families and ourselves.

To be good and successful homes, our homes must be "thoughtful" homes. They must be thoughtful both in the sense of being marked by careful thought, and in the sense of showing consideration for the needs and well-being of others. Our homes are not likely to be successful if we approach the making of them mindlessly or superficially. Throughout human history, a good home would always have required such thoughtful consideration, but the need for it is much greater now than in past generations.

This greater need for thoughtful consideration is not due to the changes in the work required to make a home. It is true that the amount of physical labor and the types of technical skills required for this work have varied and continue to vary widely across time and place. I don't need to use an outhouse, as my great grandmother might have done, but I must keep three bathrooms clean. I don't need to care for livestock, but I must take my automobile in for routine maintenance and walk my dog on a leash. I manage no servants, but I must manage streaming services and Internet providers. The challenge of dealing with such changes is simply an ordinary part of any professional work, and always has been.

The greater need for thoughtful consideration in the work of homemaking does not come from radical changes in the work itself, but in the wider culture. In past generations, this work of homemaking was culturally prescribed. The work itself might have been more or less laborious, complicated, or time consuming. But what that work consisted of would have been clearly laid out. There would have been general agreement on what was required to make a good home, and general agreement that meeting this standard was, indeed, important or even essential. Homemakers would have learned from a previous generation what work needed to be done and how to do it, whether that meant acquiring the skills and training to do the work themselves, or learning how to hire and train and manage employees who would do it. This is not to say that this work of making a home was honored, any more than the work of carpentry or farming was honored. But what the work of homemaking was, and that it was essential, could have been taken for granted. Because the nature and importance of the home was agreed upon, the home did not have to be thought about, at least to the degree required now. Certainly, the quality of any given home was not guaranteed. Whether it was a good home might depend on the character or training of the homemaker, the support of her spouse, the adequacy of her material resources, or problems in family relationships. But there would have been clarity that this home did or didn't meet an objective and generally agreed-upon standard, and it would have been praised or criticized by the culture accordingly.

The practices of this "good home" were not only culturally prescribed, but culturally supported. This support came in the form of cultural expectations and economic realities. Consider the practice of the regular family meal. Only a few generations ago, there were few alternatives to the family meal, prepared and served at home. Restaurants were for business lunches or special occasions; takeout and meal delivery were limited to pizza and Chinese. There were few convenience foods. Because alternatives were limited, daily family meals were the ordinary reality.

The culture recognized and reinforced this with the notion of the "dinner hour," during which it was considered rude to call someone or ring the doorbell, and during which it was unthinkable to schedule a meeting, practice, or game. It was assumed that the work day and school day would end in time for everyone to make it home for dinner. If someone had to miss that meal for some reason, it might have been saved for him, kept warm in the oven. The idea that members of the family would eat different meals at different times according to their preference or convenience, however, would have been countered with the homemaker's scornful "Do you think I'm a short order cook?!" We might imagine a homemaker in the 1960s, upon reading an article about the importance of the family meal, asking herself, *What other kind of meal is there?* When this dinner hour was, who was present at the table, and what menu was served and by whom, would have varied according to social and economic differences. But the cultural reality was the same for almost everyone: a regular meal, prepared and served in the home, eaten together.

This is no longer the case. Now, in spite of being a practice which is universally agreed upon as being physically and emotionally healthy, the family meal in many (if not most) homes is not the ordinary solution to the problem of hunger. Food is cheap and we are wealthy, compared to other times and cultures. We can afford to stock our kitchens with convenience foods that even a child can prepare for himself. We can purchase takeout meals without leaving our car or have food from almost any restaurant delivered quickly to our front door. The family meal is no longer the only option. It is certainly not the easiest or most efficient option, and may not even be the most economical option. In the past it would have been countercultural *not* to eat as a family, but now the family meal must fight for existence against the expectations of the workplace, the demands of extracurricular schedules, and the convenience and ease of the alternatives. No longer expected or supported by the culture, today the regular family meal is for special occasions.

The cultural devaluing of the family meal has gone on long enough that even when today's homemaker recognizes the value and importance of the family meal, she may not have been raised with it, or trained to prepare and serve it. Her spouse, not having been raised with it, might not expect, support, or value it. Planning, preparing, and serving a full meal day after day is a shockingly complicated and laborious endeavor. For many homemakers, this work is simply not in their "muscle memory." Moreover, for many family members, it may seem impossible to get home for a such a meal on a regular basis, since no one else seems to be arranging work or sports schedules with this in mind. Consequently, for the family to gather for a regular meal, eaten together, the homemaker must choose to do something difficult, for which she has not been trained or prepared, and the family members must go against the grain of expectations at work or school, all without cultural support. This is a very difficult challenge indeed.

Let me be clear: today's homemaker is not less willing or able to do difficult things than her predecessors were. The modern homemaker does very difficult things. For example, she fairly routinely separates from her babies, leaving them in the care of others. In any era, it is painful and difficult for a mother to be separated from her infant, and that it remains painful and difficult is clear from the social media posts such mothers make as they prepare to return to the office when their maternity leave comes to an end. This separation of mother and baby has always been difficult and painful, but it is currently culturally supported in a way that it once was not. Putting infants in daycare is supported by cultural expectation and economic reality, whereas the regular family meal is not.

What is true of the family meal holds true for many other practices and routines of the good home. Our grandmothers were able to step into a whole set of culturally supported routines, practices, and attitudes. They did not have to think about whether they would insist on dinner together as a family, or when the laundry would be done, or at what age their child would be allowed to access social media. They could assume, in most cases, that what had taken care of the human needs of their grandparents and great grandparents would also take care of the human needs of their own families. Until recently, the nature of that home would be something prescribed by and learned within the culture, and the best practices of the home would be strongly supported by cultural expectations and economic realities. The modern homemaker does not have such a prescription. She may be happily free of expectations, but she is also left without cultural direction and support.

In any era, a homemaker's thoughtful consideration would have benefitted her home, for she would always have needed to adapt the cultural prescription to the individual needs of her family and their circumstances. Today, that thoughtful consideration is required not only to apply the wisdom of the culture to her family's needs, but to counteract and overcome the cultural pressures that damage the home or trivialize its importance. Even more crucially, the modern homemaker must seek this thoughtfulness in an environment which, more than could ever have been imagined by past eras, opposes the interior silence needed for thoughtful attention.

Our homes are filled with screens and noise which not only distract us, but distract those we are caring for, creating barriers between us which make it so much more difficult, so much less natural, to observe each other's needs and to express our own. The gaze exchanged in the quiet darkness before dawn between an exhausted mother and her nursing infant—surely

unchanged since the beginning of the human race—
is now broken by the seductive possibilities of the
smartphone, whether the ridiculous distractions of
YouTube or the earnest demands of our to do lists and
text messages. Simply paying attention to and thinking
about those who live with us every day now takes a level
of deliberation that would simply not have been required
in an earlier generation. This thoughtful attention is not
culturally supported in any way. Instead, it is powerfully
undermined and opposed.

And this just doesn't work. There is no denying that
as a culture our homes are increasingly unsuccessful.
Studies in the fields of education, crime, and mental and
physical health bear this out undeniably. More personally,
we know from experience that there is something wrong
with the home, and this fuels our anxiety. Too many of us
grew up in homes where, in one serious way or another,
our needs were not adequately met. We didn't eat well,
we didn't get enough sleep, we weren't trained to work
hard, we spent more time occupied and comforted by
screens than by actual human beings. Too many of us
never really learned how to share or disagree or even
play with others. Too many of us didn't learn how to make
ourselves useful, how to be relied upon, how to stand up
for what we believe, how to sacrifice our comfort for the
sake of others. We did not get the care we needed, and
so we are not confident in caring for those who depend
on us. Too many of us find ourselves uncertain and
anxious about how to meet the needs of our families.
That anxiety and uncertainty drives this book.

The home in our era has fallen on hard times. Still, the home remains a powerful idea. We still want to live in homes, we spend a great deal of time and money and labor on our homes, and we still get homesick when we are away from those homes. Advertisers promote the desirability of the home and offer a vast array of products and services for the purpose of improving and enriching our homes. But what those homes should consist of, what the nature of those homes is or ought to be, how those homes will be made, and who will make them is not agreed upon. In fact, it is not so much that we don't agree upon the answers to these questions, but that we don't even ask these questions. And we don't ask these questions *not* because we already agree upon the answers, but because as a culture we no longer seem to care. We stumble into making a home, without much thought or choice or direction. We buy a house based on square footage, length of commute, or number of bathrooms and bedrooms, but we spend very little time thinking about how we will live our life in that house, how and who will make that house into a home.

There was a time when it was not necessary to think much about our homes. The homemaker followed the practices and routines she grew up with, those the culture supported, and those that economic reality rewarded. When my mother prepared dinner and called us to the table, I am certain that her purpose was to fill our empty bellies as frugally as possible. She was an excellent homemaker, a good and intelligent woman. I doubt, however, that she ever gave much thought to mealtime as a way of helping our family spend time together, reminding us of God's loving benevolence, giving us opportunities to serve and make small sacrifices, and allowing us to relax. She did not have to intend or even be aware of these benefits of the family meal, in order for them to benefit us. The regular family meal was taken for granted by the culture, and since it was an efficient and economical solution to our need for food and nutrition, she did not have to give it much thought. In order to put dinner on the table, she still, no doubt, had to overcome a tendency to laziness and selfishness ever present in human nature, but she did not have to resist the culture in order to do so. The culture supported, rewarded, and even honored her hard work. A case did not have to be made for the regular family meal.

Today, a case *does* have to be made for the family meal. Because the family meal is not as commercially profitable as other solutions, because it is a lot of work compared to these other solutions, the regular family meal is no longer our culture's default answer to the problem of empty bellies. That regular family meal which my mother provided out of habit and imitation and conformity will no longer happen, certainly not regularly and reliably, without a case being made for it, without it being thought about.

Likewise, a case must be made for many other formerly unquestioned practices and routines and ordinary realities of the home. This is not a bad thing—despite the challenge it offers to the homemaker. As tempting as it might be to some traditionally minded homemakers, simply reproducing the home of the past, even if it were possible to do so, is not the path to making a good home. The homes of the past were not perfect, but more importantly the homes of the past are in the past. They were not organized to meet the needs of families living in the present reality. A homemaker today can choose to exclude television from her home, but she cannot choose to make a home in a world where television is wholesome. She can choose to make a home without Wi-Fi, but she cannot make a home in a world in which Wi-Fi doesn't exist. She can choose not to work outside the home, but she cannot choose to make her home in a neighborhood where all homemakers are at home as well. Making a home in this time and culture requires that we thoughtfully consider many things that did not demand consideration in the past. Making our homes with thoughtful deliberation is not optional.

Not only does the modern homemaker need to make a case for beneficial practices and routines that once were simply expected and culturally supported. She must now make a case even for the desire to make a good home at all. The idea of coming from a good home or trying to provide a good home is suspect. It sounds elite, privileged, politically incorrect. Our culture does not want to accept the fact that not all homes and lifestyles are equally able to provide for human flourishing. Our culture does not want to define or support what human flourishing looks like. Every home in every era has had to deal with the shortcomings of the culture in which it is made and the personal circumstances of those who make and live within it. Today, our culture doesn't agree on what we are aiming for in our homes and doesn't want to recognize the need to aim at all. We homemakers must think about what we are trying to accomplish in our work, in a culture that doesn't want us to think about these things, and in the face of distractions which are more powerful than could have been imagined in the past. We homemakers find ourselves in a very challenging situation, but not at all in a hopeless one.

It is within our reach to make good and successful homes. We who make the home, or who support those who do, have it within our power to create the conditions and provide the means for the human flourishing of our families in our homes. This work is complicated and demanding, but also creative and fulfilling. This work is essential to the happiness of our loved ones and ourselves, and also to the health of our families, communities, schools, churches, and nation.

The solution is simple, but it is not easy. The home today, if it is to be a good and successful home, *must* be a thoughtful home. Our homes are not likely to be good and successful unless we are deliberate and thoughtful in the making of them. A good home needs to be thought about, and it is never too late or too early for us to do so.

Chapter 8
What Do We Need?

When my daughter was seven years old, I gave her the job of rinsing and drying the dinner dishes. One afternoon, she and I were having tea together on the back porch. The tea tasted funny, we agreed. It tasted like dish soap. There was no need to say a word. I watched her face as it dawned on her that her covert labor-saving failure to rinse the teapot before drying it had concrete consequences which we both could taste. Decades later I still remember this moment as a perfect instance of how the life of the home provides for our human needs: our need to learn about the world by means of our five senses, our need to think of others and to be relied upon, our need to work and our need to rest and even our need for a simple cup of tea.

So much depends upon our homes! We have determined that the purpose of the home is nothing less than to help us learn to be human and to remain human. This explains why we are anxious. It also explains why our society finds questions of how the home should be made, and by whom, so controversial. Our work is crucial, which means the burden of our responsibility is heavy. We seek clarity and confidence in this noble work. And so, we ask, what are the human needs of those we are caring for? What do our families need?

It is reassuring to realize that human needs do not change fundamentally, because human nature does not change. Human needs, however, can be ignored, overlooked, trivialized, or even denied, for a multitude of reasons. What do we need in order to survive and to flourish as human beings? Taking time to ask and answer this question will help us determine where we are headed, map out our objectives, set our priorities, and distinguish what is urgent from what is unnecessary, giving us peace and confidence in our work.

One of my favorite sayings is that with a home-cooked meal and a good night's sleep we can accomplish almost anything! The needs of our bodies are a good place to start because, although we like to ignore them, our bodily needs are objective and fairly evident. Our bodies need food, and function better if it is nutritious and consumed in the right amounts. Our bodies need protection from the elements: shelter and clothing. Our bodies need cleanliness: we need toothpaste and hot water and laundry detergent. We also need regular and adequate sleep, and health care when sick or injured or growing old.

These material needs are obvious and—despite the arguments of paleo versus vegan, sleep training versus co-sleeping, homeless shelters versus tent cities—not very controversial. Nevertheless, even with this general agreement, there are many people whose material needs are not being met, and not for want of resources. They may live in houses that have kitchens well stocked with nutritious food and filtered water, linen closets full of Egyptian cotton sheets and fluffy towels, and private bedrooms and bathrooms for all. Nevertheless, they still don't eat regularly, floss regularly, exercise regularly, sleep regularly. Instead, they fall asleep on the leather couch after binging on entertainment and snacks from Trader Joe's. To have our material needs met, we need more than material resources: we need care. We need to be guided, cajoled, or persuaded to make good use of the resources that are offered. We need, that is, to be cared for. The home is the ordinary place where we offer and find this care, so necessary for our physical well-being.

Another material need for human flourishing is so basic that it is easy to overlook. Human beings need to be in contact with material reality. Paying close attention to material reality is what has allowed us to survive as a species, carefully reading the signs that warn of an impending blizzard, studying the qualities of metal in order to make effective weapons, feeling the baby's forehead for sign of fever, listening for the approaching footsteps of the enemy. A baby learns by seeing, hearing, touching, tasting, and smelling. We continue to learn in the same way, by experiencing the world with our five senses. Our contact with the material world, our contact with the stuff that is around us, our contact with reality, is important. It is the path not only to our survival, but the path to knowledge, truth, and beauty.

Up until very recently, the human race was awash in reality. Up until very recently, our need for contact with reality has therefore never been a problem to be solved. We could not help but be in contact with it, sometimes to a dangerous degree! But now we find ourselves living in a time that is dominated more and more by the artificial and virtual. We don't play baseball in a dusty vacant lot. We don't sit on splintered bleachers and root for the home team. We don't listen to the World Series on the radio as we rake the autumn leaves. We don't even watch baseball on television. We follow the plays on the MLB app, rooting digitally for a non-existent fantasy team. We don't experience the neighborhoods and streets of our city. We don't unfold maps, look for landmarks, or ask for directions. Instead, we look down at our phone to get from place to place. Childhood road trips once involved staring out the window and playing license plate games, but now each child is focused on the screen in his lap. The dentist's waiting room used to offer magazines and soothing music. Now it offers the Wi-Fi password. Although for a coder or an engineer the smartphone might be an excellent source of contact with reality, for the rest of us it is simply a magical and seductive (albeit useful) portal to a virtual world, stealing our attention from the actual world, while disrupting and preventing our necessary contact with reality.

It is in the home that contact with reality first happens. In a culture permeated by the virtual, the home must be the place where contact with concrete reality—with plastic Legos and folding paper maps and heads of leaf lettuce still muddy from the farmer's market—holds a privileged position. Our workplace tethers us to screens, our schools require our children to use laptops, our shops and hotels insist on QR codes and online check-in. The home is the one place where we can ensure that our families remain awash in reality, because there we have the power to insist that everyone put away the screens, unplug the earbuds, and experience reality in all of its noisy, messy, and inefficient glory.

Our homes must provide for our material needs, but our human needs exceed those of our bodies and our five senses. We are persons, with intellects and emotions and immortal souls, and this multiplies human needs far beyond animal needs. We need to learn how to talk and read and write, how to measure and add and calculate, how to reason and persuade; we need to be educated. Our inborn instincts don't provide this education; we need to receive it from outside ourselves. This education begins in the home long before a child is ready for the classroom, and it is the very rare child who can fully benefit from the rich offerings of teachers, schools, and classroom learning without the support of a good home.

We need an emotional education even more than we need an intellectual education. We need to learn that we matter. This happens in the home, by the attention we receive there, or it does not happen at all. As babies we learn that we matter when someone responds to our cries and our smiles. As we mature, this knowledge is strengthened and reinforced every time someone wants to know, even insists on knowing, whether we have finished our homework or what we did at work today. We learn that we matter when someone greets us as we come in the door, listens to us tell our story, comforts us when we fail, corrects us when we err, and congratulates us when we succeed. Learning that we matter, we feel more and more deeply that we are worthy of existing independent of what we do or achieve. Outside of the home, in school and workplace, we are valued for what we do and rewarded for what we produce. In the home, by contrast, our accomplishments and contributions, although received with gratitude and delight, are not needed to justify our belonging. In the home we gain a sense of our great and imperishable human dignity.

We need to learn not only that we matter, but that others matter, too. In our homes we learn that our words and actions have the power to help others, or to hurt them. We learn that others are counting on us to be fair, to be kind, to keep our promises, and to rinse the teapot before we put it away. A two-year-old learns to be gentle with her baby brother. A teenager learns to be responsible for his younger siblings. A father learns that his hard work matters because his family depends on it. We learn that others are not objects to be used for our pleasure or profit, but persons to be helped, appreciated, forgiven, and loved. Anti-bullying exercises at school and sensitivity training in the workplace will be useless if these lessons have not already been learned at home.

Learning these lessons is essential for human flourishing. They are taught and learned by means of human contact: by rubbing shoulders with others, by fighting for a turn, by putting up with another's choice of music, by making up a game together on a rainy afternoon. These lessons are difficult if not impossible to learn in isolation. We know the heartbreaking impact of isolation on shut-ins and neglected infants, and even in the brutal society of prison, solitary confinement is a severe punishment. Such isolation is created unintentionally by our society's empty houses, closed doors, and ever-present screens. We and our loved ones must be able to satisfy our deep need for human contact, naturally and effortlessly, simply by going home.

Finally, we human beings are intellectual and spiritual, and as such we have a deep need to wonder, to ponder, to know, and to believe. We need beauty. We might think that we have greater access to beauty than ever before, as every day our lock screen provides us with a different breathtaking image from some exotic place. Indeed, Microsoft's image of a lake is more beautiful than any lake that I have ever seen. The lighting is perfect, and the loons are in focus. But viewing an image on a screen is nothing like seeing a lake. The image is only an image. We do not see the light change; we do not hear the loon; we do not smell the water; we do not feel the chilly breeze or the muggy heat. We never feel, no matter how spectacular the image on our screen, that we are lucky to have seen it. It never *really* takes our breath away. In our modern, well-lit world, we are not able to see the stars.

Our homes cannot contain the beauty of the starry sky, the Grand Canyon, or the dome of St. Peter's. Only the lucky few can gaze at a lake from the back deck. There may, in fact, be only a few memorably beautiful things in our homes, like the china shepherdess in Laura Ingall's childhood home and the music of her father's fiddle. But it is in our thoughtful home that we are given the chance to pause and gaze and wonder, to slow down enough to recognize beauty in familiar, homely things: the shine of the hardwood floor, the curve of the jade leaf, the colors and textures of a grilled cheese sandwich. It is in our thoughtful homes that we are given the chance to notice, appreciate, and respond to beauty. In them, we learn how to respond to the beauty we encounter elsewhere: to spend a few minutes watching a glorious sunset instead of hurrying back inside to get things done, to gaze at St. Peter's Basilica instead of turning our backs on it to take a selfie, to smile back at the smiling face of our infant daughter instead of trying to capture her smile on our phone.

We crave knowledge and truth. "All men by nature desire to know," says Aristotle[4]. We need to learn about reality, what dirt tastes like and what an ice cube feels like in our hand. We need to learn about how things work, about causality. What happens when I squeeze the toothpaste tube? What happens when I grab my sister's toy? How does this clock work? How did the baby get into Mommy's tummy? As we grow, we ask bigger questions, which touch on faith: Why do I suffer? Why do I do evil when I want to do good? What is freedom, and what is it for? Why do I exist? There is a human need to ask questions and search for answers.

We will not find the answers to all of our questions in our homes. But nowhere else, in an ordinary and

---

4. Aristotle, *Metaphysics*, trans. W.D Ross (Oxford: Clarendon Press, 1924), Book I, 980a, 2.

everyday way, will we be able to find the time and space and silence and freedom to ask these questions, to sit with them, ponder them, wrestle with them. Perhaps in earlier eras, this time and space could have been readily found elsewhere, by the shepherd watching his flock or the child on her long walk to school. But like it or not, our society is noisy and busy and efficient. Only in our homes, private and personal, are we able to protect and preserve the time and space and silence and freedom needed for wonder.

We want our families to be at home. But as we ponder the importance of the home, we must not forget that the world is a glorious place! The world is made for us, and we are made for the world. Many of these human needs can be met, and should be met, out in the world: in our schools and churches and town squares, in the wilderness and libraries and museums and even, sometimes, in the vast expanse of Wikipedia and Amazon Prime. But without a good home, thoughtfully made, it is far less likely that we will have the necessary foundation to be able to appreciate and take advantage of what we find in the world. Without the support of a good home, we easily miss or misuse or misunderstand so much of the goodness and beauty and opportunity that the world offers. To be able to appreciate the world, contribute to the world, and flourish in the world, we need homes that are conducive to health and work and study and rest, homes that allow for human connection, for contact with reality, contact with beauty and truth, contact with God.

All these human needs—material, emotional, intellectual, and spiritual—are the needs of those we love. This is why we make our homes, so that those we love can survive and grow and learn and flourish. And, astonishingly, when our homes are thoughtfully made, their needs will be provided for without them even asking, without them even knowing what they need. Our loved ones will find what they need, simply by coming home.

Chapter 9
The Cultural Challenge

We have discovered our destination. Our goal as homemakers is to make thoughtful homes for our families and ourselves, homes in which our human needs—physical, but also emotional, intellectual, and spiritual needs—can be attended to and provided for. We are no longer aimless, yet we are not at peace. Our anxieties originated in not knowing where we were going, but now that we have determined our destination, we might doubt that we can get there from here. To make a thoughtful home, in our degraded culture and with our meager personal resources: Is this even possible? Having glimpsed our goal, are we to exchange our anxiety for despair?

We can find hope in the fact that we do not need to create something wholly new. Across geography and across centuries, human beings and human nature do not change essentially. Therefore it makes sense to look to past practices, routines, customs, and structures of the home, those we sometimes call *traditional*. Presumably, these practices became traditions because they were found to be useful in the care of the family. Until recently, these time-honored practices were culturally agreed upon and taken for granted. Now, if they are to help us, they must be remembered, reviewed, even rediscovered. They must be thought about. Like the family meal considered earlier, these practices may no longer be supported or encouraged by our culture. They may not even be in our collective or personal "muscle memory." Yet they are not entirely lost from our culture and our consciousness. This means that we do not need to blaze an entirely new trail.

We do have to recognize, however, that these traditional solutions run counter to our contemporary cultural tastes. The regular family meal, for example, is not a foreign concept and is still an appealing idea. At the present cultural moment, however, it is judged by many to be too inconvenient and too laborious to be a practical solution to human needs. This also holds true for many other traditional practices of the home. Our cultural values and preferences tend to undermine these practices and are a pivotal reason that these practices are slipping away.

Americans, along with much of the world powerfully influenced by America, love independence. We love the entrepreneur, the self-made man, the rugged individualist. We choose the automobile over public transportation and the single-family home over the apartment building, and we almost always desire more, bigger, faster, and better. We love efficiency. We don't like to wait, we don't like to waste time, and we want "bang for our buck."

Independence and efficiency are not, of course, bad things. They are, in fact, national virtues which have allowed for glorious achievements. But independence and efficiency have become unmoored from other values and virtues that had kept them in order, values such as loyalty, solidarity, and friendship. They have become what G. K. Chesterton called "virtues gone mad."[5]

Why has this happened? Love for independence and efficiency has always been in tension with family loyalty and stability, as American literature richly illustrates (see Laura Ingalls Wilder, Wallace Stegner, or Wendell Berry). Yet it is only recently that unprecedented wealth and innovation have allowed for previously unimaginable developments in technology, fostering the belief that every problem can be solved by money and technology, rather than by human solidarity and personal sacrifices. Our answer to tragedy is to set up a GoFundMe page. We use Ring for home security when we are out of town, instead of asking our neighbor to keep an eye on things for us. When was the last time you ran next door to borrow a cup of sugar? When did a stranger last knock on your door and ask to use the phone? Our wealth (and the poorest among us are wealthy compared to previous eras) has allowed our healthy desire for independence and efficiency to develop into a fierce and excessive commitment to individualization, untethered from the family and the common good.

---

5. G. K. Chesterton, "The Suicide of Thought", in *Orthodoxy* (New York: Image Books, 1990), p. 30.

This desire for individualization and independence shapes all of us, and affects our smallest decisions and preferences. When I was growing up in the Midwest, a cup of coffee was automatically served black, and my request for cream once provoked a response of, "Where'd you learn to drink it that way?" Now visitors frequently arrive at my home with their individualized coffee order already in hand. The freshly brewed coffee which I can offer, no matter how delicious, seems vaguely second best because it limits the options and the independence of my guests. They aren't comfortable depending on my hospitality. They don't care to be limited by what I offer nor demand from me what they feel they cannot do without.

Not so very long ago, one black telephone was a standard part of a typical home. Itself an innovation in efficient communication, it nevertheless required cooperation. Before placing a call, one had to wait for another to finish her call. One was expected to answer calls and take messages for others. Private calls were only as private as the location allowed, since the house phone was affixed to the wall. "Someone answer the phone!" "Get off the phone!" and "Stop calling my daughter!" were all commonly heard. "Where's my phone?" was a question that made no sense. Now we are each expected to have our own device and always carry it with us. We can and do make and receive calls anywhere, and never think of asking to borrow someone else's phone, not even a family member's. Smartphones have not only eliminated cooperation from our phone calls, but from many other facets of our lives. We no longer need to ask anyone for directions, listen to someone else's music, share a newspaper, or find a partner for a game of Scrabble.

Our wealth has given us a pronounced distaste for sharing. It is hard to sell a house with only one bathroom. Today, having to wait to take a shower is experienced as a hardship, as is sharing a telephone or one pot of coffee. Our love of comfort is rooted in our animal nature, an expression of our instinct to survive. We assume, without thinking, that an increase in our personal comfort means an increase in our well-being, that the more perfectly our lives can be tailored to our taste and convenience, the happier we will be. What is wrong with drinking our coffee exactly the way we like it? What's the good of waiting if we don't need to? Why should we compromise if we don't have to? The market strongly supports this way of thinking. It loves individualization because it means more sales, more production, and more profit. Where would Starbucks be if we all shared the same pot of coffee?

Yet great human good comes out of the need to share. Creativity and ingenuity are fostered when we are faced with the need to do more with less. The conflicts that naturally arise from sharing a bathroom or a car can quickly be resolved by paying for another bathroom or car. But these conflicts can also be resolved by moderating our own demands, by learning how to wait or how to make do, by becoming accustomed to taking the needs of the others into account. If our innate love of independence and efficiency is allowed to run wild in excessive individualization, our own ease and comfort will become our highest motivation. We will naturally lose interest in the home and the family. If we are not trained by life circumstances to compromise, think of others, and sacrifice our preferences for the good of the other, for the good of the family, for the common good, then the home will not be a place of human flourishing but merely of human consumption. A desire to have everything exactly to our particular tastes, combined with the wealth and technology to realize this desire, undermines and eradicates the habits and routines that once made the home an effective instrument for human care and flourishing. This way of life is certain to leave us miserable, because our shallow desires to have all things just the way we want them frustrate our much deeper desire: to have a happy home in which we and our families can thrive.

These cultural developments, enabled and normalized by wealth and technology, mean that we do not have the option of unthinkingly returning to a more traditional way of life. We may be tempted to replicate the home of an earlier era, because our modern homes don't seem to be working. We may dream of hobby farms and living off the grid, raising chickens in our backyard, and perfecting our homemade sourdough bread. But it is not possible to go back in time. Therefore, the question of whether it is or should be desirable is not one we can thoughtfully ask.

It is not possible because even when we deliberately reject them, the values and practices of our culture affect us and affect those in our care. Raising chickens in the backyard was once ordinary; now it is unconventional.

Being a "one car family" was once the standard; now it raises eyebrows or evokes pity. This doesn't mean it is impossible to raise chickens or share a car, but it is impossible to do so without giving it a second thought. These earlier ways of making and running a home were once the paths of least resistance for the society, and they seem to have served and supported a healthier home life. Like it or not, our culture has chosen different paths, paths which do not lead to our desired destination. Our paths of least resistance no longer lead to human flourishing, yet they remain the paths of least resistance. This means that they are the paths we will follow, along with our children and our friends and our children's friends, unless we rebel—unless we make a deliberate and thoughtful choice to follow a different and more difficult path.

Even if it were possible, going back in time is not desirable, because we and our children were made for the time we find ourselves in. Cultural developments which horrify and dishearten older generations are encountered more calmly by younger generations as problems to be solved, as challenges which can call forth their best efforts of creativity, intelligence, perseverance, and hope. We were made to contribute to this society, not an earlier one. We are uniquely equipped to improve it, to solve its problems, to purify it and heal it. We were made for this time, and the desire to escape it, although understandable, is not our noble calling.

And so, we return to the questions with which we began: Is this even possible? Is it possible in our time to make a home that is a place of human flourishing?

Our answer must be an enthusiastic "Yes!" We are human beings with the freedom to think and choose. No matter how deeply we are conditioned by cultural forces, no matter how hard we have to fight against destructive assumptions and habits, we do not lose our capacity to deliberate, to struggle, and to change. We have our homes, and in them we are particularly free and especially powerful to foster and support true human flourishing.

What is more, once we have made certain decisions and committed to the necessary changes, once we have begun to make our homes into effective instruments of human flourishing, our paths of least resistance will gradually change. Producing a regular family meal requires a lot of hard work. Convincing our spouse and children to make it a priority can be challenging. But once it has become a normal part of daily life, the necessary work and sacrifice, while never disappearing, becomes ordinary. We develop good habits and virtues. The family meal becomes something we enjoy, something we miss when we can't be there. Being able to count on the daily family meal makes eating fast food in our car less appealing, working late less acceptable, shopping and cooking and cleaning up unremarkable. The family meal will become, for us, the reliable answer to our need for nourishment and human contact. It will become an attractive reality, which serves to build up the culture within our home.

Countercultural though it may be, our regular family meal will positively affect the wider culture in which we make our homes. Our children will go off to form new homes with the family meal in their muscle memory. Our friends and our children's friends, sharing in our homey hospitality, will realize that such a practice is possible. Our children's coaches and employers will have to learn to accommodate the priority we give to our family meal, making it easier for other families and employees to follow our lead. Our choices are not just a matter of resisting the culture, but of elevating and transforming it.

So much that is available to us can be both useful and harmful. The smartphone is useful in myriad ways, but can be harmful if it diminishes conversation, resourcefulness, and patience. Drive-through restaurants and DoorDash are useful in a pinch, but harmful if they edge out the family meal. Wealth, independence, and efficiency are tremendously useful, but can be harmful if not lived with wisdom. With our thoughtful choices, we not only protect our families, we demonstrate for our culture how to use these things wisely and not be harmed by them. We have the opportunity and the responsibility to do what we can to make the cultural paths that lead to the good well-trodden. These paths are often challenging because they are an uphill climb. But by our choices we can develop in ourselves, our families, and our culture an ability to walk uphill. We can even develop a taste for walking uphill, once we learn from experience that the air is fresh and the view at the summit is spectacular.

It is possible to make our homes a place of human flourishing despite the challenges of our culture, because our freedom and our willingness to sacrifice make it so. Although we must tolerate a world that is largely mediated through the virtual, we are free to make our homes oases of reality. We can choose to make them places where we privilege face-to-face conversation over texting, where we express emotion with our words, our tone, and our laughter, rather than with our emojis. We can make our homes places where we see and hear real things, rather than video and audio. We can make them places where we encounter not only the experiences we have individually selected, but also those that come to us unbidden: a little brother's mood, the food put on our plate, the movie chosen for our evening's entertainment. We can make them places that serve to gather, rather than separate, those who live within. In our freedom, we can habitually put away our seductive screens and thereby open ourselves, without drama or deliberation, to experiences that, whether they delight, bore, surprise, or challenge us, will always be an encounter with reality.

PART III

The Thoughtful Home

Chapter 10
Dwelling at Home

Despite the challenges of our culture, it remains possible to make a good home. In answer to those challenges, it is vital that we make a good home, and make it thoughtfully, putting our intelligence and our freedom in the service of our family's good and of the common good. How are we to do this? Where do we begin?

Before we explore in more detail the design and organization of the thoughtful home, we must face a very basic fact. Our homes will never be effective instruments of care, will not even be true homes, if they are nearly always empty. For a home to be a good home, the residents who call it home must do more than merely come and go, using the house and its contents and services as one might a full-service hotel. If, because of many outside activities and commitments, my children and I come home only to sleep and use the Wi-Fi, I will not easily know what they need or find out what they are thinking. If my husband and I pass each other like two ships in the night, we will have few natural opportunities to pay attention to each other, listen to each other, and care for each other. If our families don't spend time at home, we will still love them and worry about them. But even constant worry will not help us to care for them—unless we are with them, aware of their moods, learning their tells, noticing that something with them just doesn't seem right. The thoughtful home is one in which those who need care and those who give care spend time with one another, dwelling together.

Dwell is a beautiful word, a serious word, a word that carries with it ideas of deliberation and stability. We do not say that we "dwell" in a campground or a motel. When we dwell in a place, we make a decision to be there and to remain there. Consistency and stability are important features of any home, essential features of a thoughtful home. If our home is to function well as the primary instrument of care for the family, then the family must be able to count on it to be solid, steady, reliable.

This is not to say that a family that moves frequently, a military family, or a family of migrant workers or corporate executives, cannot have a good home. In fact, it is all the more important for the home made in predictably temporary circumstances to be marked by the stability and consistency that will only result from thoughtful deliberation. Spontaneity is a welcome part of life, and what happens in the home is often wildly unpredictable. It is the stable and consistent framework of the home which keeps spontaneity and surprise from devolving into chaos and anxiety. The stability and consistency of the home make it possible to dwell there, and not merely come and go.

Caring for human beings, within and by means of the home, is no small challenge. Human beings are free! Homes are a human reality, and human freedom is not only one of the reasons for the home, but also one of the great challenges to creating and maintaining the thoughtful home. While my children are small, decisions about how much time they spend at home are mostly my decisions. I decide whether my toddler spends her days at home or in daycare, and I decide whether the ten-year-old comes home after school or heads off to a club, practice, or lesson. But as my children grow up, they are more and more responsible for deciding how much time they will spend at home. My husband and I are fully responsible for deciding how much time we spend in our home: what sort of employment we seek, when we will come home from work, what time we will emerge from the home office, or how often we travel away from home.

Human freedom means our family members must choose to be not only physically present in our homes, but also socially and emotionally present. I can require my daughter to stay at home, but it is virtually impossible to compel her to participate in family life and truly impossible to compel her to be emotionally present. Even if such control were within our power, one of the most important things our loved ones need is to learn in the home is how to use their freedom well. To compel and control is rarely, if ever, our best path.

We cannot and do not want to confine our family members to our homes in order to care for them! Homes are not prisons and, happily, they do not need to be.

Instead of control, we are wise to rely on attraction. Our homes can be made to be attractive, and attractive precisely to those who live there. Such homes can be places to which everyone living there, including the homemaker, looks forward to returning at the end of the day—places they like to be, places where they freely choose to dwell. The thoughtful home should be designed in such a way that being there feels good. This is relatively simple, although not easy. If a home is chaotic and dirty, full of tension, criticism, and an empty refrigerator, its residents will naturally minimize the time they spend there. If a home is empty or, because everyone there is too distracted to pay attention, *virtually* empty, its residents will be attracted to other places where there is more hope of life and attention. If the best a home has to offer is what is playing on its screens, its residents can enjoy such things just as easily wherever there is a decent Internet connection.

A home will be attractive to its residents to the degree that their needs are met there, consistently and reliably. Their needs, however, are not only for a satisfying meal or a hot shower, but for conversation and rest, for affection, attention, and acceptance, even the need to be needed. What makes a home attractive to its residents cannot be determined by an algorithm. It is the homemaker's task to determine whether for her own family peace and quiet is more attractive than high-spirited fun, and whether a clean kitchen is more attractive than homemade cookies still warm from the oven. Most of the residents, most of the time, will not themselves be making deliberate decisions to spend time at home. They have other things on their minds. The homemaker, therefore, by means of her thoughtful design and effort, has the challenge of making a home that is so appealing to her family that they naturally choose to dwell there.

In our noble desire to make our homes appealing and attractive to our families, we can be tempted to make them into pleasure palaces, in hopes of outcompeting the world for pleasures and delights. This is a fool's errand, for the world is so much bigger than our homes. Yet there are things more attractive than material delights. In high school, my son and his friends usually gathered at one boy's house. I asked my friend Gail, their generous hostess, what I needed to offer in order to make our house as attractive to these boys as hers clearly was. Did I need a bigger television screen or a pool table? Did I need a refrigerator stocked with popular snacks? She assured me that the boys didn't come to her home because of the entertainment offered there. They came, rather, because they knew that they were welcome. What did she do to make them feel so welcome? She told me that whenever her son asked whether his friends could come over, she almost always said yes, even though it often meant changing her own plans. Whenever they came over, she offered them her homemade cookies. Her simple and reliable hospitality made these boys feel welcome, and that feeling of welcome was what kept them coming back.

Our families will freely return to our homes, spend time in our homes, dwell in our homes, not because they are pleasure palaces, and certainly not because they are prisons, but because by our thoughtful work we make them places of welcome and loving attention. Knowing from experience that at home they will find good food, a pleasant atmosphere, and someone who is happy to see them, they will not have to make a deliberate decision. Heading home will be their default. Coming home will be, if not the path of least resistance, at least a truly inviting path. When our families truly dwell in our homes, rather than using them only as refueling stations, our thoughtful homes can foster their human flourishing simply because they are there.

The home itself—its physical design and contents, its routines and practices—should make it easy and natural, the path of least resistance, for those within its walls to be awash in reality and beauty. If a home is filled with beautiful artwork and the aroma of brownies, filled with good books, a crackling fire, and family photos, filled with Grandma's overstuffed rocker, a piano, and a Boston terrier, then those who dwell in that home will be formed and influenced by those things. The screen of a smartphone is seductive, and ingeniously designed to be so, but a Boston terrier and brownies still warm from the oven are seductive, too. And they are real.

The thoughtful home should function to gather together those who are, as individuals, dwelling there. This is part of what distinguishes the home from the hotel. A hotel might be attractive, in that it promises a hot shower and a comfortable bed at the end of a long day. A high-end hotel might offer beautiful décor and excellent room service. But a hotel does not gather us together. In fact, the nicer the hotel, the more we expect not to be disturbed. We do not want our homes to function like hotels, providing for certain material needs but keeping residents apart. A successful home is, by accident, tradition, or intentional design, one that tends to gather people together and keep them together, whether around the fire, the kitchen table, the jigsaw puzzle, or the bathroom sink.

This togetherness runs counter to our cultural ethos. We are encouraged to desire privacy, personal space, and individualized service, and to seek such things for ourselves and for those we care for. In my pleasant neighborhood, the houses, built in the first half of the twentieth century, are small by middle-class standards—fewer bathrooms and bedrooms, less closet space, and smaller kitchens—than the families who now can afford these houses have been taught to want and expect. My neighbors with one or two children knock out walls and expand up and out the very houses in which, only a couple of generations ago, families raised six or seven children. Their taste for space and privacy demands this.

A certain amount of space and privacy is conducive to human dignity, yet we will do well to organize our houses and the family life within to minimize isolation and increase human contact. The physical design and habitual practices of the thoughtful home will guide people into the same space at the same time, regularly and frequently and as a matter of routine. They do not have to be called to a family meeting or required to show up for roll call. If dinner is served at one place and one time, the family will naturally gather. If bedrooms are shared, roommates will gather for a bedtime story and bedtime prayers when they are young and share thoughtful or playful conversation as they grow older. If a table is kept clear and available for a game, those looking for something to do will gather there. If there is room on the couch for everyone to gather to watch a show, entertainment will more easily be a shared pastime.

Our efforts to create a thoughtful home will be fruitless if those who live under our roof spend their days alone, behind a closed bedroom door, absorbed by the private entertainment of their own screens. In making our homes we should look for ways to draw our family members out of their private spaces and into a shared life. The thoughtful home facilitates a life lived in common, a life which fosters human fellowship and nurtures the conviction that each one of us matters and that each one of us is needed, valued, and loved.

We need to give time to pondering these questions and putting our ideas into practice, discovering, often by trial and error, what works and what doesn't work, reviewing and revising our plans in the light of these desired outcomes. What makes my home attractive to my family? What makes them (and me!) want to be there, choose to be there, and even sacrifice their individual preferences and conveniences to be there? What kind of interior design and household habits serve to gather them together routinely, making positive human contact the ordinary experience of life at home? What kind of furnishings and habits of the home put my family in contact with reality and beauty? What aspects of my home will serve my family, simply because they come home? Such a thoughtful home is an excellent instrument for flourishing, making it not just possible but probable that those dwelling there will find what they need to do so, both at home and out in the world.

Thoughtful homes need homemakers, not just for their planning and pondering. Their presence is needed. For our homes to be places where our families choose to dwell, we homemakers must choose to dwell there, too. We must be there, and we must be there in a particular way. We must be there thoughtfully. What does this thoughtful presence require?

The homemaker is the one in the home primarily responsible for paying attention to others' needs, giving thought to what they need and the best way to fill those needs. To carry out this work thoughtfully, the homemaker must be in the home with time adequate to the scope of her project. How much time is adequate? Surely there is no universal answer to this question. The lives of thoughtful homemakers will vary as widely as individual families and cultures vary one from another. But whether she lives in a three-bedroom rambler in the Midwest, an elegant apartment on Park Avenue, or a grass hut in Africa, the homemaker needs adequate time to carry out her project. Adequate time is not "barely enough" time to do the cooking and the laundry, but time enough to spend with those who live in her home, to be available to them and to pay attention to them, to notice things, to think things over, to come up with plans, and to carry out those plans. Time enough for all these things.

When my son was little, I began to realize that he would start misbehaving when his father had been unusually absent or distracted due to work. I wondered whether his behavior might improve if I could find a way for the two of them to spend some time together. When my husband came home from work, I suggested to him that, because our boy seemed to need a little "Daddy time," he play Legos with him rather than chatting with me while I made dinner. The difference this made was immediate. The problem was small, and the solution was easy. But my time and presence had been required: time with my son to recognize that his behavior had changed, time spent thinking about what might be going on, and time to consider a remedy. Had I had only "barely enough" time to get home and fix dinner, I might have misdiagnosed the problem—or reacted to it with frustration and anger.

How much time is adequate? The answer to this question will vary widely depending on the number and ages of those living in the home, the temperament and energy level of the homemaker, the amount of help she has, and other factors. Certainly, much of this necessary attention and thought can happen while the homemaker's hands are busy with other things. She can pay attention at the dinner table. She can notice things while supervising homework. She can think things over while driving to work, especially if her attention is not diverted to her smartphone or dulled by lack of sleep. The precise amount of time required to make a thoughtful home will vary, but adequate time is required regardless.

Our culture and our own hearts are not generous in finding and safeguarding this time. Is it not true that we often shortchange the family meal for the sake of outside activities? That we easily give up the sleep we need, so crucial for patience and cheerfulness, to meet a deadline at work? These are difficult negotiations, but we must arrange our own lives and our families' lives in such a way that this essential requirement of the thoughtful home, the requirement of time, is given pride of place.

Time is our treasure. As a culture we give great importance to saving time. Yet far more important than saving time is spending our time wisely. We should spend our time on the things that matter most. We should spend our time on and with those we love. We should spend our time generously on our homes and in our homes. There is no other way to have a thoughtful home.

While we are at home, whether all day long or after a demanding workday, we must be truly present there, paying attention. We homemakers cannot afford to be chronically distracted. We need mental space for thinking about what is going on around us. In every era, it has been possible for the homemaker to be physically present in the home but emotionally distant, mentally distracted, or simply focused only on herself. Such a homemaker, like Charles Dickens' Mrs. Jellyby or Jane Austen's Mrs. Bennett, is a stock character in both comic and tragic novels.

Today, this timeless temptation has been multiplied enormously because of an unavoidable digital world intentionally engineered to dominate our attention to the exclusion of the actual world around us. The distraction and isolation that historically would have required physical separation or even mental illness can now easily be our ordinary state of being—and by our own choosing. In order to make a thoughtful home, the homemaker must be willing and able to pay attention to her home and those who dwell there.

We must be present in our homes, body and soul, if our homes are to be thoughtful homes. It is our presence in the home that makes this possible. More than anything else, our presence makes our homes attractive. That is so not because of our beauty or the power of our personalities, but because we are there, paying attention to the others, listening to them, thinking about them, and taking care of them.

We may do this work primarily, but we do not do it exclusively. Ideally, everyone in the home participates to some degree in this work and thoughtful deliberation. Collaboration in the work of thinking about others and attending to their needs, including the needs of the homemaker, should be fostered and encouraged. But our collaborators—spouse, children, hired help—will learn how to do this and be led to do this by our example, instruction, and leadership. Our mission as a thoughtful homemaker, for our families and for ourselves, calls us to be generous with our time and our attention, often heroically so. Our mission begins with learning how—with all of our other responsibilities, professional commitments, and passions—to dwell in our homes.

Chapter 11
How Do We Do This?

Making a home is a wonderfully practical endeavor, but perhaps my patient but practical readers are beginning to say, "Enough, already!" I agree. As necessary as it is to identify principles and clarify goals, there comes a time when we must put down our book and get dinner started. Our principles must be incarnated in the material reality of our home and in its way of life. We have identified our destination, and this gives us confidence. When we didn't know where we were going, we weren't ready to plan an itinerary. Now that we know, it is time to choose our path.

And so, what will we do? *How* will we make a thoughtful home? What am I going to make for supper? What am I going to bring into my home? What objects, attitudes, and habits, so that my family will thrive, so that my baby will sleep through the night, my little boy will do his homework, my husband's blood pressure will even out, and my daughter's broken heart will mend?

What will I promote or discourage, require or forbid, so that my family will flourish?

Figuring this out is perhaps the greatest challenge of making a home. Cultural attitudes and technology have changed so rapidly and so dramatically that we can't necessarily rely on what our mother did decades before. We aren't foolish enough to do whatever Google suggests. Making a home, therefore, is a work which requires paying attention to the details, collecting and analyzing the facts, listening to our intuition, consulting trustworthy experts, and coming up with a good plan. Our work is to observe and question, patiently mulling things over, identifying problems and concerns. Our work is to come up with possible solutions, discussing them with our spouse, our friend, our doctor, our mom. Our work is to make a plan, give it a try, and see what happens. Our work is to analyze the results of our trial, relieved and grateful when something works, patient and curious when it doesn't.

This challenging work can be one of the greatest pleasures of making a home. Far from being trivial or tedious, it is work that requires sensitivity, curiosity, creativity, and intelligence. Although practical and mundane because it is so intimately concerned with the concrete details of ordinary life, its scope is vast and its impact is unlimited. This work is nothing less than the creation of a culture.

This work is not about making and enforcing rules. We are not seeking the magic formula which will prevent anything bad from happening in our families. We are free and our families are free, and bad things will happen despite our best efforts. The daily family meal does not guarantee that good conversations will be frequent and eating disorders avoided. Excluding the Internet from our bedrooms does not guarantee that our families will get the rest they need and be protected from pornography. But the thoughtful homemaker's choices and plans allow a healthy culture to form in a natural way.

Years ago, I worked with a young woman from Kenya. Whenever we had to do business by phone, she would preface the conversation by asking after each member of my family, with whom she had only a passing acquaintance. Although I found it charming at first, I soon became impatient and frustrated by her solicitude. To my mind, we had business to do and we were wasting time—time which was not ours to waste. Getting straight to the point felt sincere and responsible to me. Getting straight to the point felt rude and disrespectful to her. This is the power of culture.

Such differences reach down to the tiniest details. As I opened a new jar of salsa in my kitchen, a helpful house guest moved toward the recycling bin with the empty jar. Without a second thought I grabbed the jar, and transferred the remaining tablespoon of salsa into the freshly opened jar with a rubber scraper. He looked at me, confused, and asked me why I would scrape out the jar when I had a fresh jar at hand? I looked back at him, equally confused. Why would I toss out a tablespoon of perfectly good salsa? We had been raised in different homes, and what was second nature to me was odd behavior to him. What would never have occurred to him to do, would never have occurred to me *not* to do. This, too, is the power of culture.

Culture is the way of life shared by a group of people, consisting of the behaviors, beliefs, and values that they accept (generally without thinking about them), passed along to them by the example and approval of cultural leaders. In our homes, unless we yield this role to others, we are the cultural leaders. What we promote and exemplify will affect how those in our homes will tend to think, what their values and priorities will be, what they will spend their time doing and talking about, how they will tend to react to opportunities and setbacks, and how they will choose to deal with an empty jar of salsa.

Our son once observed that although his home had only one television and no video games, almost every room contained a comfortable chair, a good reading light, and a bookcase full of books. Almost every evening for twenty-five years, my husband or I could be found reading to a child in our home. Both the material contents and the way of life in our home meant that there was never a need to insist on the value of reading. By means of small daily decisions and small daily actions, a culture of reading was firmly established.

Good conversation in our homes cannot be required or demanded, and it certainly cannot be purchased. The stage, however, can be set for it. Comfortable seating in a common space will help to draw people together. Shared habits of treating one another with respect help everyone to express themselves openly, listen attentively, and respond thoughtfully. Training in etiquette and firm control of phones allows conversation to flow without interruptions. These practices contribute to a culture of good conversation, which means good conversation will arise naturally.

Such a healthy culture is built up of small mundane details, decisions about how to arrange the furniture, where to charge our phones, and what to make for dinner. We gather up our observations and our insights, our experiences, our tips and tricks and recipes and routines, and we weave these things together to build up a healthy culture within our home.

The thoughtful homemaker does not adopt practices and methods randomly or impulsively. She selects and evaluates them based on whether and how they contribute to making her particular home a place of human flourishing. Will they bring her family, including herself, into closer contact with reality, or will they be distractions from it? Will they strengthen the human relationships in the home, or will they be obstacles to unity and fraternity? Will they form in the family a taste for beauty and truth, a willingness to sacrifice, a desire to know and serve God? This is what it is to make a home.

The power of the home is why the homemaker labors for her home, worries about her home, and loves her home. The home that she labors to make beautiful and orderly will form those who dwell there to value and desire beauty and order. The home that she fills with books, art, and music will lead her family to think of books, art, and music as a normal and necessary part of ordinary life, rather than something found only in classrooms and museums. The home that she has arranged so that her loved ones live closely with others will liberate them from focusing too much on themselves and encourage them to think about what serves the others.

Because these practices are challenging, we are best served by establishing them as early as possible in our homes. We might be tempted to think that we don't have to worry about any of these things until we have children old enough to notice. Yet a homework ban on Sundays will be much easier to impose on a child who has never known otherwise than on one with a settled habit of procrastination. That homework ban will make more sense if there is already in the home an established culture of Sunday as a day of rest and leisure. Although the time will surely come when it dawns upon a child that she does not have to follow this practice, she will by that time have become accustomed to the pleasures of a leisurely Sunday. She will experience working on Sunday as a loss, rather than as the status quo.

These practices and methods should be discussed by bride and groom when establishing a new home so that there is clarity and unity between them as family leaders. The life in the home will flourish if there is such unity. With unity, husband and wife are able to support each other; when one begins to tire or despair, the other can persevere and encourage. Difficult and challenging times in the life of a family—whether the sleepless chaos of postpartum life, the stressful worry of unemployment, or the emotional challenges of the empty nest—will be much more easily navigated if good habits have already been established.

Although starting early in the building of a culture is ideal, it is not always a family's reality. Although a unified vision of the purpose of the home is ideal, this, too, is not always a family's reality. There is always room for hope, however. It is always possible to change, and it is always possible to change for the better. These effective practices are great matter for ongoing conversation and deliberation throughout the life of a marriage, a family, and a home. Identifying and implementing these thoughtful practices is a huge challenge, and it is no wonder that we feel anxious and overwhelmed by the magnitude of the project.

Thankfully, we do not have to start from scratch. Whether our homes are wealthy or materially deprived, made for a large young family or for a couple of empty nesters, made in an urban apartment or on a family farm, there are common methods which will help to make our homes good homes. There are practices and designs that, in almost any home, will result in a material setting and way of life that is more physically and emotionally healthy for those who live there. There are practices and attitudes that, in almost any home, will minimize isolation and maximize freedom and responsibility, and that will tend to privilege the actual over the virtual. There are common practices that make it easier for the homemaker to be with those in her care regularly, frequently, and thoughtfully. There are common practices, designs, and ways of life that, adapted thoughtfully to the particular circumstances of a particular home, will make any home—large or small, rich or poor—a useful instrument for the human flourishing of those who dwell there.

In the following chapter, we will consider some of the methods and ways of life that have shown themselves to be effective means for making successful homes. These traditional practices have rarely been imposed by civil or religious law, yet they have been widespread across time and geography. Homemakers are a practical people with little time for pointless activity. For these practices to have become widespread and enduring, they must have proven themselves to be useful. These methods, supported by custom and tradition, have stood the test of time.

They have stood the test of time, that is, until now. Most of these practices are fading, the result of our consumer culture's extreme commitment to individualization, efficiency, and comfort, as well as our culture's preference for novelty over tradition. They are fading rapidly but they have not entirely disappeared. Most of us have some familiarity with them, if not from our own childhood, then from literature, television, and movies. Most of us are even able to see the wisdom of these practices. Nevertheless, their countercultural nature tempts us to dismiss them as impractical and unrealistic.

We are foolish to dismiss these practices without thoughtful consideration. They came to be common practices because they served some end. More often than not, they served several ends. They may have been adopted by our forebears more by convention than by deliberation, but they became conventions in the first place because they were useful solutions to the challenges of caring for a family. We should ponder all the benefits of a given practice before we discard it as unnecessary, impractical, or unrealistic. When we do need to discard it, we should make sure that the needs it once answered are being provided for elsewhere by other means. We no longer need to make a daily visit to the village well, because we all have running water in our homes. But that laborious and inconvenient trip to the well was also a daily opportunity for conversation among women otherwise isolated by their circumstances. In the absence of the camaraderie of the village well, we need to find other places to fill our social needs—perhaps by getting off our phones and out of our cars to chat with the other parents waiting in the school pickup line. With FaceTime available, handwritten letters are no longer the easiest and most efficient way to keep in touch with those we love. But if we always choose efficiency, our grandchildren will never be able to discover a box of love letters from their grandparents' courtship. Is this a loss we are willing to bear?

The work of making a thoughtful home is as difficult as it is noble. *Prudence* is the name for the work of figuring out what we are trying to accomplish in and by means of our homes, and of choosing the best methods for accomplishing it. Prudence is the virtue that helps us to discern the true good in every circumstance and to choose the right means of achieving it. We will not be able to make a good home without growing in this virtue of prudence.

Philosophers tell us that one essential step in making a prudent decision is to take counsel, to seek the advice and example of those with wisdom and experience before making and acting upon our own decisions. Reconsidering traditional practices of the home is not an exercise in nostalgia. Our effort to identify and consider the methods and designs that have been common to homes across cultures and across centuries is a practical and effective way of taking counsel from our homemaking forebears, a way of prudently enlisting their help in our shared project of making and keeping thoughtful homes.

Chapter 12
Methods for Making a Thoughtful Home

Human beings exist in space and in time. This is a requirement of our existence so absolutely fundamental that imagining otherwise is beyond our power. This reality of our corporeal nature does not change, but modernity has gradually but powerfully eroded and distorted our practical experience of space and time. The seasons still change; the sun still rises earlier in the summer and snow still piles up in the winter. But electric lights and attached garages mean these changes have little practical impact on our daily lives. The telephone has made our voice as easily heard by someone two thousand miles away as two feet away.

Ironically, the more "connected" we have become, the more disconnected we are becoming. Technology has reduced our need to move through space: to bike to the library, walk to the mailbox, or push a cart through the grocery store aisles. Modernity distorts our sense of time: we don't have to wait for the newspaper to find out the election results, wonder for a week about what will happen next on our television show, or estimate how long it will take to drive to our destination. Our computers have accelerated this detachment from space and time so much that we now speak easily of "virtual reality." We accept this disconnection and distortion easily, but without an awareness that it is changing us.

We will, of course, never escape space and time. Our smartphones take up space and scrolling on them takes up a great deal of our time. What we call "virtual reality" is actually real. Our devices are real and computer technology is real, as real as sound waves and the daily revolution of our planet. But our altered experience of space and time in this digital form is disorienting—as anyone knows who has tried with thumb and forefinger to "zoom out" a paper map or even the intricate tattoo on someone's skin. Inevitable as these changes may be, we are beginning to notice how this altered and diminished experience of space and time is not making us—and those we love—happier. Our altered experience of time is not yielding more time for us to enjoy actual reality. Our altered experience of space is not bringing us closer together.

The thoughtful home is rich with remedies, beneficial to both body and soul, for our diminished experience of time and space. These remedies are sometimes in the form of exclusion and control. Video games might be excluded from a thoughtful home, and smartphones collected at the door. But the most effective and enduring remedies of the home will be those that help to develop a taste for reality: a delight in seeing and hearing and smelling and touching actual things, a comfort level with face-to-face conversation, and a desire for being with others in person. A child who has grown up playing card games around a table, experiencing the banter and laughter and hot chocolate, will not be satisfied by Zoom meetings and online Scrabble. A child who has felt the painful pleasure of her frozen hands starting to thaw after coming inside from a snowball fight, or one who has stared at a fire while listening to a good book being read aloud, will never be satisfied by images and experiences confined to a screen. One who has long been accustomed to being looked at and listened to will find the divided attention of someone absorbed by a screen frustrating, if not offensive.

For the sake of human flourishing, one of the best things the home can offer is a rich experience of the human reality of space and time. As we consider, or reconsider, the methods and practices that we will adopt in our own homes, we can do so according to how they impact time or impact space within the walls and life of our homes. These methods will be effective because they help us, in time-honored ways that benefit the family, to manage either the space of our home, its material contents and design, or the time in our home, its routines and schedules.

The Queen

The regular family meal is the queen of these best practices because of how powerfully and regally it reigns over both the material reality and the temporal reality of the home.

When I was in college in the 1980s, our food service had two dining styles, offered on different days and for different meals throughout the week. One was cafeteria style, with which any college student is familiar. The other, employed for most weeknight dinners, was called "family style." At family style dinners, we sat with each other around a table, and only one menu was served. The meal was brought to the table in serving dishes which were passed around the table, each diner serving himself from the common dish. When everyone at the table had finished, a student waiter would be signaled to clear the dishes and bring dessert.

These family style meals were a remarkably different experience from cafeteria style meals. Family style meant that we all faced the same food, whether enticing barbequed chicken or overcooked spaghetti, together. We all faced each other, sitting around a table. Our meal was an event with a beginning, middle, and end, and despite some late arrivals and early departures, we could usually count on spending thirty minutes or more with one group of friends, eating, chatting, and relaxing, arguing, flirting, and complaining. These meals were not fine cuisine, and I think we generally preferred the food that was served cafeteria style on the weekends. But the family style meal was about something more than food. It was about a shared life, one that formed habits of submitting our individual preferences to a common experience and yielded rich conversations and deep friendships.

This institutional adoption of the family meal speaks to the cultural power of the common practices of the home in an earlier era. Sadly, but not surprisingly, this dining experience is no longer a feature of the dining plan at my *alma mater*. It passed away years ago in the wake of food sensitivities, scheduling preferences, and a cultural lack of interest in, even distaste for, living a shared life.

Of course, my college dinner was never truly a family meal, only "family style." The true family meal happens in the home around the family's table, at an hour and with a menu chosen by the homemaker according to her abilities and resources and the needs, tastes, and availability of the family. The dinner hour might change according to the changing schedules of the family, but the dining companions remain constant—changing only as new family members are added, others grow up and depart from the home, and guests temporarily enrich the family gathering.

The family meal may no longer be imitated in institutional settings. Yet it remains not only possible but supremely useful as a "best practice" in the thoughtful home. It is an efficient and economical way to feed our families. But its benefits for the thoughtful home increase precisely to the degree that it is about something more than food—that it is about a shared life that forms habits essential to human happiness.

What happens at this family meal? Why is it such a precious opportunity for giving and receiving care? Of course, those gathered around the table are offered the food that they want and need, with which both their hungry bellies and their nutritional requirements can be filled. Those gathered at the table are also offered a rich and steady encounter with material reality, the different tastes, smells, textures, and visual presentation of the food, as well as the gleam of silver, the flicker of candle flame, the texture of linen, and the sound of laughter. This sensory contact with reality provides a daily training for them in being open to new experiences, appreciating good things, and cheerfully accepting things they do not like.

Many practical skills can be taught and practiced in the context of the meal, both at the table and in the meal preparation and the cleaning up afterward. We teach and learn, by instruction and practice, how to use a fork gracefully, carry a glass of water without spilling, butterfly a chicken breast, or fill a dishwasher. We teach and learn, by example and discreet correction, good manners and self-control, how to wait to start eating until everyone has been served, how to keep our elbows off the table and our napkin in our lap. Because the meal is regular and frequent, these small skills can be acquired gradually, eventually becoming second nature.

Our common need for human contact is richly met at every family meal. Parents and children, often apart for much of the day, are given the opportunity to sit down together, learn one another's news, and gradually deepen their knowledge and understanding of one another. This is a gift especially for the father or mother of the family who must be away from home all day absorbed in professional work. It affords a convenient and dependable opportunity to attend to his or her family.

Gathered together at the table, everyone has a chance to share and to serve by setting the table, helping the baby into the high chair, and passing the salt. The family meal offers a simple and natural opportunity for praying together, and for celebrating feast days, birthdays, and milestones. In the course of the meal, everyone can practice the art of conversation, learning by example and by experience how to listen, how to tell a story, how to offer an opinion, and how to challenge an opinion in a respectful way. Those who can't or don't want to contribute to the conversation—whether toddler, surly teen, or exhausted adult—will still be present, observing, absorbing, and being noticed.

When the family shares meals together regularly, not only are they reliably fed, but they also have a natural and regular experience of fellowship without the need for calling awkward family meetings or synchronizing schedules for a family game night. When such meals are frequent and habitual, the members of the family find themselves together for hours each week, side by side and face to face, not because they are obligated, but for the simplest of reasons: because they have to eat, and they want to eat. This supremely useful gathering happens again and again because, again and again, the members of the family find themselves hungry, tired, and ready to sit down with people who care about them.

Volunteers in the Jesuit Volunteer Corps, living together in intentional households, are advised that, regardless of whatever else they do or don't do, if they eat at least five meals together each week, they will achieve a real community. If they eat fewer than five meals together, they won't. With regard to the family meal, more is better. Breakfasts together set the tone for the day, and lunches together, for those at home, offer a midday chance to rest, refuel, and recalibrate. The shared meal is so important to the thoughtful home that it should be rare for anyone to eat alone. Even when someone has had to miss dinner, another can be asked to sit with him while he eats his warmed-up meal, providing a little of the company and attention he has also had to miss.

The impact of daily family meals extends beyond the dinner hour, coordinating the life of the home all throughout the day. Children know that they can usually find Mom in the kitchen before dinner if they need her advice, and that Daddy will be more likely to play a game with them after the rest and restoration of a good meal. These regular meals organize and punctuate the family's days. It is natural to think of getting this task done before lunch or waiting until after dinner to attend to that.

Such meals are a great deal of work for the homemaker. Indeed, the required planning, shopping, cooking, and cleaning up generally make up the greatest part of her practical work. The family meal requires of everyone sacrifices of time, availability, and personal preference. Yet these meals, served as frequently and regularly as possible, are worth the effort and the individual sacrifices. It is a wonder how comprehensively the regular family meal can take care of the physical, emotional, intellectual, and spiritual needs of each member of the family.

Living in Time

The management of time in the home is concretized in daily and weekly routines. Unlike the routine of the typical workplace, the routine of the thoughtful home is not fundamentally concerned with efficiency and productivity. Although the homemaker will often follow a daily, weekly, and seasonal plan for her housework for the sake of efficiency in caring for her house and its contents, efficiency is not the primary consideration of the thoughtful home.

The key purpose of a routine in the thoughtful home is to make it not only possible but likely that family members will spend time together. This is fundamental because if family members are rarely in the same place at the same time, there is little opportunity for human contact, little opportunity for them to be challenged, encouraged, and corrected, hugged, teased, and put in a headlock. And most importantly, there is little opportunity to be attended to, understood, and cared for.

Until relatively recently, sunrise and sunset dramatically synchronized the daily routines of all who dwelled in the home. One had little choice but to rise and retire with the sun or gather after dark around the light of the fire or the oil lamp. Everyone's workday would have been determined by available light. Although our schedules are no longer determined by the sun, it still serves a family well to rise and go to bed in a coordinated and habitual way. Being well-rested is a key to human flourishing, and regular bedtimes and rising times greatly improve both the quality of our sleep and the likelihood that everyone, under normal conditions, will get the amount of sleep necessary to thrive. Ordinarily husband and wife will rise earlier and retire later than their little children do. If the two of them rise and retire together, they will not be like ships that pass in the night, two individuals independently trying to survive the burdens and chaos of family life. Instead, they will have regular opportunities to talk and plan together and to enjoy and benefit from each other's company and support.

If the temporal reality of the home is anchored by common rising times and common bedtimes and punctuated by common mealtimes, then the life in the home can easily and naturally include common times for doing homework or chores. The temporal life of the home is further enriched by doing certain things in a certain order. We get dressed before coming down for breakfast. We clear our places after we finish eating. We do our homework after eating a snack and before going outside to play. Such coordinated routines in the home create not only peace, but natural opportunities for human contact and encounter.

If the custom in our home is to hang up our coats as soon as we come inside, then the coat closet becomes a meeting place. It becomes a place of service as my husband takes my coat to hang it up before hanging up his own. The children who tumble out of the car naturally find themselves together in the mudroom, laughing and teasing, waiting for their turn, helping the littlest one to reach the hook. In addition to encouraging order and the care of our possessions, such a routine subtly contributes to the shared life and culture of the home. The family life happening in the mudroom is so natural that no one realizes that it is helping them grow in order, understanding, service, and love. Such temporal routines, which are often called "rules," make it far more likely that those who dwell in the home will connect not only at the dinner table, but also while jostling one another at the sink in the morning, studying together around the kitchen table, and cuddling against each other while sharing a story at bedtime.

The purpose of these common routines is not that everyone will do everything together, or that everything will happen at the same time and in the same way. The organization of time in the thoughtful home should not be ordered to regimentation or primarily to efficiency. Regimentation is not helpful in forming a family in healthy human freedom. Undue emphasis on efficiency undermines the message that we care about one another because of who we are, rather than because of what we achieve. Rather, such temporal coordination means that it is ordinary, not unusual, for family members to be home at the same time, even in the same room at the same time, so that their lives are naturally enriched by human encounter and naturally filled with opportunities to give and receive attention and care.

It is true that routines that guide us into the same place at the same time will often give rise to noise, minor conflicts, and small inconveniences such as children whining in the car or a quarrel over whose turn it is to choose the movie. Our culture leads us to treat such things as problems to be solved with another purchase or a digital distraction. The thoughtful homemaker will be wise to consider noise and inconvenience not always as problems to be eliminated, but rather to be accepted as the ordinary effects of a shared life, even welcomed.

The good effects of a daily routine in the life of the home are multiplied by a coordinated weekly routine. The anchor of the weekly routine is the practice of living Sunday (or another day depending on religious tradition) as a day of worship and rest. On this day, the family worships together and puts aside, for the sake of leisure and rest, such work as can be accomplished on other days. Our contemporary culture prefers to treat weekends as a time for sleeping when we want, doing what we want, consuming what we want, and only begrudgingly attending to chores and homework when forced by the looming reality of Monday morning. This contemporary pattern simply does not serve us as effectively as did the weekly routine of our forebears.

Although our culture no longer observes the "Lord's Day" in principle, it is still possible to make it a day of rest in our homes. For most of us, Sunday remains a regular day off from school and work. It makes sense for us, regardless of our religious practice, to preserve what is left of these shreds of cultural tradition, protect them from the further encroachments of youth sports tournaments and work emails, and even try to recover lost ground. A common day of leisure and rest spent with family and friends is a great good, both in our homes and in our culture.

Such a weekly rhythm is well worth the effort. For those who are not accustomed to refraining from work on Sunday, the learning curve can be steep, but the reward is tremendous. Sunday becomes a day to look forward to, rather than the day when leftover obligations from the previous week must finally be faced. With work completed before Sunday dawns, it becomes natural and convenient, a path of least resistance, for the family to spend the rest of the day going on outings, playing games, watching a movie, and working together to accomplish chores that can't be set aside. In a shared culture of Sunday rest, joining with other families for meals or recreation or service is easy to schedule. Sunday reclaimed in this way gives us the weekly luxury of time for doing those things we never can find time for, like visiting someone in a nursing home, teaching a child to ride a bike, or reading in front of the fire.

A Sunday lived in this way will help to synchronize the rest of the week. If Sunday is a day free from work, then homework and household chores will fall to Friday afternoon or Saturday morning, providing more opportunities for connection and a common life. But again, this is not about regimentation. A shared day of rest does not mean that family togetherness is mandated. If the rhythm of the week is shared, family togetherness will not *need* to be mandated. The shared daily and weekly routine of the home makes it inevitable that we find ourselves together at work, play, and rest, naturally experiencing the emotional and material benefits of rich human contact. The discipline of refraining from professional work and homework whenever possible on this day creates a welcome oasis from the burdens and toil of the week, richly answering our human need for rest in an irreplaceable way.

The very possibility of organizing our time to meet our family's needs presupposes a private and personal family home. Those who live in institutions do not have the ability to organize their time according to their private needs. Meals and work and recreation will happen in an orderly way, but according to the goals and policies of the institution rather than the wise and free deliberations of love. We have minimal control over school and work schedules. But in our homes, we have the ability to create a schedule, routine, and set of practices that contribute to the flourishing of those we care for. Such a home must be, increasingly, a thoughtful home—one not organized carelessly according to current trends. It may be true that "no one else does homework on Friday!" But it can also be true that in *our* family, in *our* home, *we* do. When we wisely organize the way time is spent in our homes, we privilege human contact and preserve time for the work, recreation, worship, and rest which is so beneficial, even necessary, for our human flourishing.

Our Space and Our Stuff

The home is a material structure, organized to meet the human needs of those who live within it. Now we turn to consider this material structure. This structure absorbs a great deal of the resources of the homemaker, both her money and her labor. This structure is about provision and protection. By means of bricks and mortar and a watertight roof, by means of deadbolts on the door and parental controls on digital media, the home protects the family from weather and wild animals as well as from cultural pressures and trends which are not healthy for us. The material structure of the thoughtful home protects family life from the public eye. Although the home is opened in hospitality to those who do not dwell there, it is opened according to the decisions of the family and not according to the demands or curiosity of the public. Our homes should not be fortresses and cannot be sterile environments. They should, however, be places where what and who is allowed to enter is either beneficial or, if potentially harmful (the wild neighborhood kid, the controversial presuppositions of a popular show, the disembodied voice of Alexa), able to be safely tolerated or thoughtfully remedied by the healthy life within.

The structure and material reality of the home is for provision as well as protection, and these two purposes are intimately related. In a good and thoughtful home, experiences and conditions that might otherwise be destructive can be rendered positive and enriching because of the formation offered in the home. Children growing up in a materially impoverished home can become insecure and materialistic, or they can become strong and resourceful, made confident by an early life that was both poor and good. A wealthy and luxurious home can produce adults who expect to get their own way in everything, or adults committed to a life of love and service. The healthy formation which makes the difference is provided not only from the instruction and example of the parents, but also by the material reality of the home itself. If a home has nothing much to offer beyond a great Internet connection, then turning away from a screen will always be experienced as a deprivation. If a home is filled with interesting and beautiful things and with attentive and loving people, then turning away from that screen will be rewarded in manifold ways.

The material structure of our home creates a private space and further divides that space according to the needs of human dignity. Even within private family life, our human dignity requires private spaces for our private needs. We need bathrooms and bedrooms where we can bathe, sleep, and change our clothes in privacy, and we benefit from other spaces where we can find quiet to pray and ponder and work with concentrated focus.

The same human dignity that calls for such private spaces must also be protected from harm. To this end the private spaces of the thoughtful home must be kept free from things and people that are either dangerous, overwhelmingly attractive, or both. In an earlier time, parents might have worried only about keeping the amorous boyfriend from climbing the rose trellis to their daughter's chamber. Today, simply by closing her door, it is easy for a child to close off her bedroom from the loving supervision of her family while opening it recklessly to anyone who desires to enter by means of social media.

For decades now, a key practice of the thoughtful home has been to prevent access to the Internet in private spaces. This was easier to accomplish a generation ago, when children weren't required to use laptops for their homework, and when we didn't carry smartphones in our pockets. For the sake of their human dignity, our families must still be protected from the Internet.

How we allow digital devices to be used in our homes is of crucial importance. This demands thoughtful policies, heroically enforced. We must give careful consideration to practices such as parking all smartphones at a charging station when at home, having a common place and time for doing any homework that requires a laptop, and using parental control applications and programs consistently and attentively. Because of the ever-changing nature of technology, our policies will themselves require constant and thoughtful review. This is part of the challenge and responsibility of making a thoughtful home.

A tremendous help in this regard, so ordinary and "old-school" that it is easy to overlook, is that whenever possible and appropriate, private spaces should be shared. Although every mother longs for the private heaven of a locked bathroom door, it isn't good for anyone in the home to be habitually hiding out alone behind closed doors. Shared private spaces mean that the privacy of these spaces is conditional. Sooner or later, someone will shout through the bathroom door, "What are you doing in there? It's my turn!" No teenage girl can be isolated in her bedroom for long, if her mother can send her roommate in with orders to "go check on your sister." Before making expensive plans to add bedrooms and bathrooms to our homes, we should give thought to how smaller homes naturally draw both children and adults into the demands, benefits, and protection of shared family life.

Complementing its private spaces, the structure and design of the home provides family spaces: living room, dining room, playroom, kitchen, porch, and yard. These family spaces are not exactly private—no one knocks before entering—but are still protected. They are protected from public access—freed from the intrusions and distractions of the outside world—for the sake of the family life of the home. Perhaps it would be more accurate to say they are *freed for* family life, and thus made available for rich and fruitful encounter and interaction.

To foster this rich and fruitful family life, our family spaces should be comfortable and inviting, more so than our bedrooms. It is not beneficial for family life if bedrooms are the only places to relax. We want to organize and furnish our homes so that wandering into the kitchen or the family room is reliably rewarded with pleasurable family life. Whenever possible, our common spaces should have comfortable furniture and pleasant lighting, and attractive features like a fire in the fireplace, space to play games or do puzzles, or the means to share music, movies, and stories. These places should be marked by a good human tone which makes it pleasant to be in them, an expectation that conduct there will be marked by respect and informal good manners. Large families are a big help in ensuring that there is family life going on in these family spaces. But even in small households, we homemakers can foster such family life by being generous with our time, inviting the others to keep us company while we cook dinner, join us for the show we are watching, or sit down next to us on the couch to chat.

We make these family spaces more attractive with policies that privilege face-to-face interaction over any kind of virtual interaction. When someone in the home receives a call or text, this is no different from a knock on the front door. The public is asking to enter the private family home. Of course, there is nothing wrong with answering a doorbell. But we should not let such a request interfere with our dinner hour, bedtime, or family game or movie. Likewise, we must not allow the notifications on our phone to distract or isolate us from the human being sitting across from us at the table. We cannot afford to put the family spaces and family life in our home at the mercy of the public's desire for our attention.

What do we put in these family spaces? A demanding but helpful mantra is William Morris' famous dictum: "Have nothing in your houses that you do not know to be useful, or believe to be beautiful."[6] This is especially helpful if we understand "useful" to mean useful for human flourishing. To make a home in accord with such a dictum requires thoughtful deliberation. A coffee mug is useful, and it can be beautiful. Twenty-three unmatched coffee mugs are neither useful nor beautiful; they are clutter.

---

6. William Morris, "The Beauty of Life," a lecture before the Birmingham Society of Arts and School of Design (February 19, 1880), later published in *Hopes and Fears for Art: Five Lectures Delivered in Birmingham, London, and Nottingham, 1878 — 1881* (London: Ellis & White, 1882, p. 108).

A popular magazine that claims as its mission to help us live a "real simple" life is little more than a thick catalog of advertisements for things we can acquire. Our consumer culture trains us to assume that every problem can be remedied by some purchase: an Instant Pot, a Roomba, a closet organizing system, an app on our phone. This thoughtless habit of trying to solve problems by acquiring something new not only drains our budget and clutters up our homes, but also changes our feelings about the things in our homes. We "adore" our new appliance or our new app for a few days or weeks or months because of how it is changing our life. Sooner or later, however, it begins to dawn on us that this purchase has been more of a distraction from, rather than a remedy for, the inescapable problems of the human condition. We begin to resent the space it takes, the maintenance it requires, and the sense of failure it calls forth in us.

We do not need to be minimalists by any means. We simply need to be thoughtful. We should consider thoughtfully what furnishes and fills and makes up our homes. Do these things help our families to flourish, or are they an obstacle to that human flourishing we are trying to foster? Are these things useful? Are they beautiful? When our useful things can be beautiful, so much the better!

We want the things in our homes to be things that will lead us higher: good books, musical instruments, or a crucifix over the door. We want the things in our homes to bring us beauty, the way paintings, music, fresh flowers, and candles on the table do. We want the things in our homes to bring us together: comfortable seating in the living room, an ample dining room table, a swing on our front porch, a cozy spot in the kitchen where someone can sit and chat while we cook.

Whenever possible we want our things to tell a story. A comfortable chair is good. If that comfortable chair is also beautiful, it is better. But if that chair was a wedding gift to Great Grandma, if it is the chair in which Grandma rocked Daddy as a baby, if it is the chair in which our children remember being cuddled and read to, then that chair is a treasure. Such a chair favors not only our comfort, but our memories and our dreams. The fossils on the coffee table are no prettier for having been purchased at a souvenir shop in Wyoming rather than from Amazon.com. But they contribute more to the life of our home because they remind us of our first family camping trip.

Our ordinary everyday things will be both useful and beautiful when they are arranged and used with order and care: onions and garlic in a basket, glassware on a shelf, towels folded and stacked in the linen closet. We treat the things in our home with respect, using them for what they are designed for, putting them where they belong when we are done with them, repairing them when they break. When the material contents of the home are kept in order (provided that "keeping order" does not itself become a disordered mania), life in the home will be more tranquil and attractive.

Order is attractive, and order also makes work and family life more feasible. A table piled high with mail, cereal bowls, and abandoned projects will not gather the family around it. A clean, bare table draws the family irresistibly because of its obvious potential as a place for a game of Scrabble, for doing homework, for rolling out cookies, or cutting fabric for a quilt. The material order of the "stuff" in our homes becomes ever more important as actual reality must compete more and more with virtual reality. In virtual reality, clutter never seems to be a problem; surely this is part of its attraction. Television screens never need to be cleared off before they can be used, and computer screens can be cleared by the click of a mouse. Virtual reality is therefore always ready to be used, ready to draw us away from contact with a more beneficial, but messier, reality.

The arrangement of things in our homes matters beyond basic order. Careful thought should be given to what is placed in a room and where in the room it is placed. I have a comfortable rocking chair which is "my spot." It is where I once nursed babies and where I now pray, read, plan menus, and make lists. It is where I take my coffee break. My family has learned that they can find me there. If I put that chair in my bedroom, I am usually left alone when I am in it. If I put it in our family room, I become more available to my family regardless of my occupation. If I place another comfortable chair next to it, I often am joined by a companion when I sit down to take a break. The way we arrange our things sends a message. Furnishing many rooms with a bookcase and a reading light communicates that reading is valued in this home. Allowing a family room to be dominated by an enormous television screen communicates that in this home family life is dominated by passive entertainment.

Having no place in the home where the family can watch a show together communicates that in this home such entertainment is a private pursuit, not a part of family life.

The thoughtful homemaker might be tempted to react against the materialism and consumer mentality of our culture by disregarding the importance of the material goods which form and fill, enrich and sometimes clutter her home. Many make the mistake of trivializing the contribution things make to the life of the home. Such a reaction might lead her to make her purchases chiefly according to short-term cost and convenience, not wanting to waste her resources and mental energy on mundane realities. But it is human beings who dwell in our homes, not angels or beasts. Our bodies and souls, the material and the eternal, are so intimately united that mundane realities—what we listen to and sit upon and eat—have eternal consequences. As such, we are formed, for good or for ill, by those things which surround us every day, those things that form our choices, imaginations, and memories. Our space and our stuff matter.

By considering, or reconsidering, these "best practices" of earlier eras, we should not be under the illusion that our forebears lived in better or healthier times. The cultures that formed them were as deeply flawed as the culture that forms us and our families. We look to these practices not because they come from a healthier culture, but because they have been found in and endured across many cultures and eras. These ways of life have stood the test of time not because our forebears were wiser than we are, but because their cultural circumstances did not allow them to so easily dismiss or trivialize that which is daily, ordinary, and of the earth.

Our human cultures vary widely and change quickly. In all this change, however, there are two constants. Our human nature does not change, and so as human beings, material body and immortal soul, our most fundamental human needs remain constant. The second constant, intimately related to the first, is that the home is where the culture, always powerful and always imperfect, is most effectively transmitted, purified, and elevated. The home is not so much a fortress as a filter. We homemakers know the importance of attending to the filters in our furnaces and vacuum cleaners and fish tanks.

When we clean the living room, vacuuming and dusting and polishing, the last step of our work is made up of small details: moving the furniture back where it belongs, fluffing the sofa pillow, straightening the painting on the wall. This work is ordinary, but it is far from trivial: we are preparing and maintaining the setting of our family's life and of our own life. We know that our work matters because it touches human lives. We know, if we are thoughtful, that our homes matter because those who dwell there matter, matter to us and matter eternally.

Chapter 13
The Work of Making a Thoughtful Home

During a certain period of my life, I was regularly asked to give talks to parish women's groups. Like the remuneration, the stakes were pretty low, but my talks were well received, and I enjoyed the work. One evening, I drove out of the city to give a talk at a country parish. Because the talk was sponsored by the Knights of Columbus, I probably shouldn't have been surprised to find only men in the audience. Despite my dismay, I gamely started in, delivering my talk as written to what turned out to be a distressingly unresponsive room. I slogged steadily onward until, halfway through my prepared text, I glanced up at the man who had introduced me standing at the back of the room. Pantomiming the cutting of his throat, his message to me was unmistakable: "End this now!" That evening was a turning point for me. I realized that I really was not, nor would I ever be, all things to all men, or even to all women.

Unlike the Knights of Columbus in that parish hall, however, you are not a captive audience and you are still reading. That is likely because you are a homemaker, you plan to become one, or you want to support and understand one better. Although the home is of great importance to every human being on the planet, the ideas presented in this book are of most immediate interest and value to homemakers themselves.

Our definition of the home requires an agent, which we have called the homemaker. We need clarity about this term. Is *homemaker* the name for anyone doing certain types of activities? When we say that a driver ran a red light, *driver* says nothing about the agent except that he was operating a motor vehicle. In this sense my husband could be called a "homemaker" while he is drying the dishes. Or is *homemaker* a personal identity, less about what I do, and more about who I am?

The most helpful way to think of the homemaker, for the purposes of the thoughtful home, is as a *professional*—like a professor, an actor, or a waitress—and to think of homemaking as a *profession*. To say someone is a "professional" says more than that he is doing a particular activity. When we say that a *professional* driver, whether a school bus driver or a Formula One racer, ran a red light, we know a great deal more about the driver and the import of the situation than that he was operating a motor vehicle. To consider homemakers professionals does not mean that they are paid for their work. Mark Zuckerberg received no salary as CEO of Facebook, but he was not therefore an amateur. George Washington accepted no salary as commander in chief of the Continental Army, but was in every respect a professional soldier.

To think of homemaking as a profession rather than a personal identity means that we do not have to choose, at least in theory, between being a homemaker and working professionally outside the home. Because professions are not mutually exclusive, we can easily imagine someone being both an actress and a waitress. Exercising both professions at the same time might be exhausting, but also professionally fruitful. Her acting skills might help her to be a better waitress, and the wide experience of human nature which she receives from waiting tables might enrich her acting. Certain professions will combine more easily than others due to their practical demands, and certain people, due to their temperament and stamina, will find combining two (or more) professions more possible and more appealing than others will. In principle, however, it is possible for someone to work at multiple professions, so long as he or she has the time and personal capacity to meet the professional requirements of each.

If we consider homemaking to be professional work, our question is not how *exclusively* a homemaker must dedicate her time to making her home, but whether she has *enough* time and availability to do so. This profession is more than a list of tasks, like vacuuming the living room and getting the laundry done, to be checked off. It calls for being in the home for enough time—and with enough mental focus and emotional recollection—to carry out the indispensable work of paying attention to and caring for the others. While practicing another profession, will the homemaker be able to be in her home and with her family for enough time and with enough attentiveness to see and understand their needs and to arrange for those needs to be met? Every homemaker must answer this question for herself. How she answers it must be based not only on the numbers and neediness of those in her care, but also on her physical stamina and mental health, her general efficiency, her powers of observation and intuition, her temperament and taste, her family's economic resources, and the support and participation of her spouse in the project of homemaking.

This question should be faced with honesty, bearing in mind that other forces in our culture work steadily to draw our attention away from our homes and diminish our very capacity for paying attention. This question must be faced with courage, bearing in mind that our own hearts are not generous in finding and safeguarding such time. We might frequently stay up late to meet a deadline, thinking that we have no choice, without considering how our lack of sleep will make us cranky and impatient with our families. If a homemaker is perpetually exhausted and distracted, it will be almost impossible for her to be thoughtful.

We count on our family's resilience, reminding ourselves that generations of families before ours have faced extreme challenges of poverty, war, and cultural chaos and came through unscathed. "We were poor, but we were happy." In very many cases, however, the resilience of children and families came from their deep sense of being cared for and attended to in the home. This is a difficult calculation, one that can often be determined only by personal experience. It nevertheless remains a professional requirement of the homemaker to make decisions about career and family in the light of this essential requirement of time and attention.

Fortunately, the thought and attention required of the thoughtful homemaker can happen while her hands are busy with other things. In graduate school, unmarried and feeling the burden of my studies, I fell to chatting with a fellow student who was older and many years into the work of raising a family. I asked her how she managed to keep up with both her home and her studies, apparently successfully. She thought a bit and then said, "Well, there's a lot of time for thinking while stirring the pudding."

It is true that there is a lot of time for thinking while folding laundry, pulling weeds, commuting to work, and stirring the pudding. There is time and opportunity for paying attention while driving carpool, or while drying the dishes our child is washing. Part of the appeal in recent years of baking our own bread and raising chickens in our urban backyards comes from the opportunities these projects provide for us to be in our homes with time to think and listen and observe. Buying our bread in a store takes us away from our home, and ordering our bread online requires a kind of electronic focus which takes our attention away from those in our care. (If you do not think this is true, consider how you react to a child's question while you are trying to place an online order compared with how you might react to her same question while you are kneading dough.) Baking our own bread is in no way a requirement for, nor a guarantee of, a thoughtful home! But our increasingly efficient, convenient, individualized way of life diminishes such opportunities for the habitual thoughtfulness and attention which give us confidence and serenity in this professional work.

Do we not long to be confident and serene in making and keeping our homes? Deepening our understanding of homemaking as professional work, and working at it professionally, is the key to increasing this form of "job satisfaction." The homemaker will be much more successful, confident, and serene if she thinks of her work as professional work and approaches it as a professional.

What do we mean by doing something professionally? What are the practical implications of treating homemaking as a profession? In practice, we often distinguish professional work from other work which is "just a job." Sometimes we describe this sort of work as mindless, something in which we merely do what we are told, for the money or just to get it done. Our professional work, on the other hand, is work we have trained for, work we care about and make an effort to improve in.

Like other professional work, making a home requires learning and developing a body of knowledge and skills, meeting objective professional standards, and putting in hours of practice. Like other professional work, the homemaker benefits from the coaching, support, and the camaraderie of professional colleagues: her mother, her friends, Julia Child. With the help and support of these colleagues, she applies her training, talent, and hard work to a complicated and constantly changing project.

If a homemaker thinks of her homemaking merely as an endless to-do list, she will do only enough to get by, distracting herself from the problems and challenges inherent in her work rather than seeking solutions and developing her skills. Her home will not be thoughtful, and she and her family will suffer for it.

A professional approach liberates her from viewing the demands of her work as unfair. The homemaker is at times confronted with very difficult working conditions and unsustainable demands on her time and energy: when she is pregnant or postpartum, when she has three children under the age of five, when her spouse travels a lot, or when there are deadlines and pressures from her other professional commitments. During these periods, she is prone to feeling unappreciated, misunderstood, and hopeless. She experiences frustration, even desperation, at her inability to accomplish what the others need and expect from her. Whatever circumstances may be, they still need dinner, and clean underwear, and someone to listen to them. At times like these, she is often driven to see her situation not as difficult and unsustainable, but as unfair. "Why do I always have to be the one to notice the sticky kitchen floor, to get up at night with the crying child, to make dinner (and so on)?"

In most respected professions, there are seasons or situations in which the work is extremely challenging to the point of being unsustainable: accountants as tax deadlines approach, restauranteurs on Valentine's Day, physicians during residency, teachers in badly run and underfunded schools. Unlike homemakers, however, these other professionals seldom perceive their work as unfair. They may burn out, but they do not cry out, "Why do I have to be the one?" It would be highly unprofessional for a hospital intern to complain to his patients about his situation, no matter how sleep-deprived he is. If the homemaker views the work of the home as just a job that someone has to do, as the inescapable work with which she has been saddled, she will easily feel resentful and hopeless. But if she sees the work of the home as her profession, she will approach it with a sense of responsibility.

When her work becomes overwhelming, it is part of being a professional to seek solutions and look for support and understanding more from those who share her profession than from those who benefit from it.

The homemaker's professional challenges are real and formidable, and they are best met with a professional approach. Every profession has its own inherent challenges, which are almost always better addressed by those who work in the profession than by outsiders. These inherent challenges can be welcomed as professional opportunities for creative problem solving, solidarity with others in the profession, and personal growth. Finding better ways to meet these challenges and sharing these solutions with others in the profession elevates the entire profession.

The profession of homemaking differs from many other professions in terms of working conditions and expectations. On the one hand, the homemaker has no contractually defined work day, no time clock or "quitting time." She has no defined job description, no salary, no performance review, and no expectation of a raise or bonus for her professional sacrifices. She is not motivated by the hope of promotion or the fear of dismissal. There is no boundary between her workplace and her home. She may work with constant interruptions. She may often be assumed to be available for family and social life throughout her workday because her work is not taken seriously by others. In many respects, her professional work is similar to that of an entrepreneur who runs her own business, and yet she does not have the clarity of the "bottom line" to tell her whether or not she is succeeding. On the other hand, the fact that the homemaker does not have a boss, a contract, or a human resources department means that she has great freedom to shape and regulate her work environment to suit her needs and her family's needs.

A professional approach to the work of making a home benefits from clarifying which tasks and responsibilities are part of this work. Each homemaker might do this in a different way, but a thoughtful distinction between her professional work and her part in the life of the family is helpful. For example, she might consider preparing dinner for her family to be the work of the home but joining her family at the dinner table to be family life. Doing laundry and planning menus would be professional work, while diapering the baby and reading to a child would be family life. Occupations such as homeschooling, organizing the Cub Scout fundraiser, or running a Pampered Chef business would be neither the work of the home nor family life, but would fall into a third category of "working from home." There will be a great deal of overlap among these categories. The thoughtful homemaker will be paying attention to the needs of her family (part of her work) while eating dinner with them (family life), and a trip to the grocery store with preschoolers is essential to the work of the home, but it is also a family outing. These distinctions are more theoretical than actual, but making such theoretical distinctions helps the homemaker to realize that her professional work is not as endless and overwhelming as she might have believed.

Distinguishing her work from her family life will help her to define her workday. A professional workday should have a beginning and an end. Perhaps she considers her workday to begin when she throws the first load of laundry into the washer while the coffee brews, or when she starts preparing breakfast for the family. Perhaps it ends when she finishes the dinner dishes, or even earlier once her children are trained to handle this job. Perhaps her circumstances demand that she put in another two hours of work after dinner but allow for an extended break during afternoon naptime. The homemaker will be much happier in her work if her workday doesn't begin the moment she gets out of bed and ends only when she collapses into bed at night. It is fully within her power to affect this. It is true that, as in some other essential professions, she is almost continually "on call." How often she is called away from leisure, family life, or other professional work in order to bandage a skinned knee or deal with an overflowing toilet will vary considerably throughout her homemaking career. This is simply one of the challenging aspects of this noble profession.

Approaching the work of the home professionally requires working in a professional way. Like other forms of professional work, the homemaker should endeavor to carry out her work with order, intentionality, and constancy. At certain times in her homemaking career, as when she must work with several small children underfoot, she might be unable to do such constant and sustained work for more than an hour at a time, or even a quarter of an hour in extreme circumstances. Nevertheless, working in this way should be one of her professional goals. That the homemaker carries out her work while caring for small children, while caring for the dependent elderly, while not feeling well, or while vacationing at her lake cabin, is part of her working conditions and a unique professional challenge. Such challenging working conditions, however, will be made more bearable—not less—by striving to work in a professional manner.

All professional work requires study and training, and homemaking is no different. A homemaker who enters the profession already skilled in cooking, housekeeping, and running a budget will be at an advantage. Like many other professions, however, there is no substitute for actual experience in the field. Approaching her work from this point of view helps her to welcome challenges as opportunities to learn, improve, and grow professionally.

In almost any profession, we need to study aspects of management to advance. We learn how to hire, train, and support those who work under our leadership and authority. Those working under the direction of the homemaker might include a house cleaner or a babysitter. Most importantly, it includes those family members who live in the home. Part of her professional approach will be to evaluate how each member of our household can contribute to the making and keeping of the home, and then train them and hold them to a realistic standard. Whether the homemaker does this in a regimented way or in an atmosphere of informal affection will depend on the homemaker and her coworkers, but it ought to be done. The homemaker who complains, "Why do I always have to be the one?" often suffers due to her lack of attention to the management aspect of running her home.

I remember a period in my mother's life. Every day, after cleaning up the breakfast dishes and finishing the morning's housework, she would take a coffee break with Marge from across the street. As children, we were always happy when Marge came over because we knew that our mother would be in a better mood once the coffee cups were drained and the conversation concluded. Marge was not only my mother's friend, but her professional colleague.

Our colleagues are one of our most important professional resources. These colleagues might be our mother, our housekeeper, an author, or a podcaster. Our very best colleagues, however, are those fellow homemakers who are also our friends. We depend on them not only for recipes and dry cleaner recommendations, but for wise counsel and a shoulder to cry on. If we turn to them regularly and deliberately as experienced and thoughtful colleagues, we will find great support and camaraderie in our uniquely challenging professional work. With them, we can and should pose our questions: How do you get your work done when you are up at night nursing a baby? How often do you change your sheets? How do you get your husband to pitch in? How do you balance traveling for work with the needs of the home? We can learn both from those who are in very similar situations to ours—those making a home with many small children, or on a very limited income, or while working full-time at another profession—and also from those in different circumstances, such as older and more experienced homemakers.

The homemaker, whether she works outside the home or not, frequently suffers from a feeling of isolation. So much depends on her, and she is alone with this responsibility and workload. Her work outside the home might give her minimal opportunities for spending time with her homemaking colleagues, or her small children might give her little freedom for doing so. But time spent in deliberate conversation and consultation with such colleagues is not just a luxury; it is a solid and important professional support. Finding these colleagues and making time for these conversations is part of the work of making a thoughtful home, part of building up a network of professional connections, solutions, and support. The ideas presented in this book could serve as a starting point for many such conversations between homemakers.

Both adequate time and a professional approach are fundamental to making a thoughtful home successfully and with confidence. Are there circumstances, however, in which making a thoughtful home is not possible? Perhaps you recognize that things need to improve in your home, but you have resolved more than once to cook dinner every night, declutter your house, or institute a regular family game night, and more than once you have failed. You are discouraged, and beginning to believe that it is unrealistic to think that someone like you— disorganized, or comfort-loving, or easily distracted, or not at all "domestic"—will ever be able to carry through with these kinds of changes.

To you I say: try giving these ideas a little more thought. More than anything else, the thoughtful home is about paying attention to and thinking about what your family needs. You are the one who is best suited for this job, regardless of your strengths and weaknesses, because you are the one with the desire to care for them. This work is not all-or-nothing. If you try something and it doesn't work, you have not failed. You have learned something about yourself or about the situation, or both. Think about why that experiment didn't work. Troubleshoot and problem-solve. Talk to your professional colleagues, that is, call your friend or text your sister. With a few adaptations to suit your circumstances and a lot of patience, your persistence in one or two small efforts will almost certainly bear fruit. One of the glories of human nature is that we can always change, and we can always change for the better.

Perhaps you have found that your family refuses to cooperate with these ideas and recommended practices. Well established in bad habits of the home, your husband and children have no interest in making or cooperating with change. They think they are happy with the way things are, and do not share your anxiety. To you I say: don't give up. Play the long game. You might not be able to succeed in instituting a daily family meal, but you might be able to get them to warm up to a Sunday brunch. Something is better than nothing, especially when it is offered with cheerful affection and a sense of detachment from the outcome. You are planting seeds that may take root and grow, but only bear fruit far into the future. No effort, however, will be wasted.

You might think that your case is special. You have so many very small children. You are so completely overwhelmed by the chaos they create, that you can't possibly find the time or the peace for deliberation and planning. You have teenagers, rebellious and confrontational, who have no interest in being at home. You are an empty nester, and your home no longer seems to be a vital concern. You might even think that none of this pertains to you because you do not have a family home of your own: you live alone, or with roommates, or in your parents' home.

If you think you are a special case, you are absolutely right. Every home is unique. Every homemaker has her own challenges. Yet it remains true that every human being needs care. It remains true that the home is the best instrument for providing for the unique (or not so unique) needs of the human beings who live there. It remains true that the home is the ordinary means to human flourishing. You are the one who, thanks to your thoughtful deliberation and heroic effort, can make a home perfectly tailored to your own special case.

The work of making a thoughtful home is difficult—physically and intellectually and emotionally demanding—and especially so during certain periods of a homemaker's professional career. It requires intelligence, creativity, flexibility, stamina, patience, and perseverance. This work is necessary for the human flourishing of those who are closest to us, essential to their happiness and to our own. This work, well and thoughtfully done, contributes in turn to the good of our extended families, our neighborhoods, our communities, our culture, and our nation. This work, because of its difficulty and its importance, is noble, honorable, and even heroic.

Nevertheless, this work goes unnoticed and unappreciated. It is famously taken for granted. And yet, is this not the nature of work in general and of professional work in particular? Although we might occasionally thank a soldier in uniform for his service, in general, we take it for granted that our soldiers are standing guard. We take it for granted that our farmers are raising and harvesting the food that we need, that our truckers are transporting it, and that our store owners are running the grocery stores where we will find and purchase it. We take it for granted that engineers are maintaining our water treatment plants. We take it for granted that nurses and doctors will be waiting to help us whenever we need to go to the emergency room. We depend on these professionals, and we count on their professional work. The more professionally they do their work, the more we are able to take their work for granted. Like all professionals, homemakers can be proud to be counted among the ranks of such unsung heroes.

Chapter 14
Where Is God in the Thoughtful Home?

Every few years, due to my husband's professional work, I leave my Minnesota home and travel to Rome, to make our home there for a few months. It is not easy for me to grasp the antiquity of Rome, for in Minnesota the oldest building is not yet two hundred years old. In fact, I have heard my eighty-five-year-old house referred to as an historic home.

My favorite church in Rome is the Basilica of San Clemente, which has been standing for nine centuries, gloriously decorated with a stunning apse mosaic and cosmatesque floors. St. Thomas Aquinas could have worshiped in this church. This ancient building, however, is only the most recent of the churches that have occupied this site. Underneath this basilica, there is an earlier church decorated with columns and wall frescoes dating from the fourth century—not long after Christianity was legalized in Rome. St. Augustine could have worshiped here. Deeper still, beneath the fourth-century church is a large set of rooms with herringbone floors and tufa walls, a Roman villa at least two thousand years old. History tells us that this villa served as a house church in which Roman Christians worshiped illegally. St. Paul could have worshiped here.

The villa is thought to have belonged to a Roman named Titus Flavius Clemens, and before it was a church and in addition to being a church it was a home. Where is God in the home? In Rome in the first centuries after Christ, God was in the home in a literal way: Christian worship and religious instruction in this young and illegal religion took place in homes, in particular, in Clemens's home. I like to think that Clemens's home was a thoughtful home.

What about today? Although faith and worship are at the center of my life, *The Thoughtful Home* is not fundamentally a project of religious faith. I have tried to write a book which is not oozing with religion because the home, like the family, work, and friendship, is an essentially *human* reality. As such, it is shared by everyone, important to everyone, regardless of religious belief and practice. Not all homemakers want to factor God into their home equations. Some may not want to include God in their homes because they reject religion, or do not find it valuable or interesting. Others may believe that although God is important, he is someone we visit at church rather than include in daily life. Because the home is a human reality, thinking about the home without reference to God, regardless of the reason, does not render the homemaker's conclusions pointless or futile.

On the other hand, although *The Thoughtful Home* is not a religious project, God is as much a part of the home as he is a part of every other aspect of human experience. He is not just a part of reality, but the source and summit of reality. Our human flourishing requires that our spiritual needs be attended to, along with our physical, emotional, and intellectual needs. I am confident that many of my readers share this belief. If I write about human flourishing and contact with reality and do not bring God into my reflections, such readers will not be satisfied.

Consequently, this consideration of the place of God in the home will be for some readers the summit to which the previous fourteen chapters have been building. Others might think of it as optional—interesting reading, but not relevant to their anxieties, concerns, and goals. I'm good with that. And so, in that spirit we ask, Where is God in the thoughtful home?

What are the spiritual needs of human beings? The Universal Declaration of Human Rights defends the right of every person to manifest externally his religious belief in teaching, practice, worship, and observance. For a family of faith, there is a need for their home to express their religious identity and remind them of it. That can take many forms: a print of Albrecht Dürer's *Praying Hands* above the sofa; a *mezuzah* on the doorpost; a statue of St. Francis in the garden; a prayer card taped next to the kitchen sink. The organization and use of time in such a home will include time for religious observance: prayer together before meals; worship on Sunday morning; Sabbath rest. Religion and belief can be manifested in every aspect of the home culture. If there are bookshelves in the home, some of the books will be about God. If there is art on the walls, some of that art will have a religious theme. A musical family will include in its repertoire Christmas carols, gospel music, or Beethoven's *Missa Solemnis*. The family meal will recognize religious holidays and seasons: a festive menu on Christmas and Easter, meatless meals on Fridays of Lent, or a special dessert on the feast day of someone's patron saint. The clothing worn, the entertainment enjoyed, the language used in the home will all be in harmony with the religious beliefs of those who live there.

The spiritual needs of the human person, however, are more fundamentally met in the home in an interior way, that is, by the ways that the structures and routines of the home form the human person to be receptive to and capable of faith and religious practice. This interior formation happens, albeit unintentionally, even in those thoughtful homes in which religion is not practiced. If we live in a home, for example, where things happen in an orderly and regular way, it will be much easier for us to make a place in our daily life for time with God.

When my husband and I were newlyweds, our first conflict was over something very silly. I would prepare breakfast and put it on the table, but he wouldn't join me until he had finished his morning prayer. I was grateful that my husband was a godly man but, with Flannery O'Connor, I believed that God is better thanked by eating our food hot. We irritated one another until we discovered a simple solution: we set a time for breakfast. Now he could start his prayer early enough to be done before the eggs got cold. A chaotic home does not infringe on religious freedom or destroy religious belief, but it makes regular religious practice more challenging.

If we live in a home that fosters contact with reality, we will be prepared to understand our faith more readily. The Bible is filled with images, metaphors, and parables. Our experience with yeast and salt, with mending cloth and whitewashing a wall, with borrowing from a neighbor, lighting a candle, and sweeping a floor prepares us to understand Sacred Scripture. We can learn about these things in Sunday school, but our religious understanding will go much deeper if we have experienced these things from our earliest days. Contact with reality not only widens our experiences but deepens our grasp of causality. What happens on our screens appears both magical and inconsequential, but our daily contact with reality teaches us that something does not come from nothing, that our actions have consequences, and that what we do matters.

Both philosophy and divine revelation teach us that God is Truth, Goodness, and Beauty. What we have in our homes, what we do in our homes, day by day, year by year, builds up in those who dwell there a taste for truth, goodness, and beauty. When we watch a movie together and we ask afterwards, "Was that true? Does life work that way?" we develop a taste for truth. This is the same as a taste for God. When we see the beautiful painting every day because it hangs in the dining room, it forms within us a desire for what is beautiful, and therefore a desire for God. This contact with reality even forms us to grasp, in our limited human way, what we can never fully grasp: that God's existence is his essence, that he is the great I AM. The ubiquitous virtual world can eat away at our grasp of what it means for something to *be*. Our homes, brimming with reality, are the antidote.

If we live in a home where human contact is privileged and fostered, where we are regularly and frequently with mother, father, brother, and sister, as well as with babies, sick people, and guests, we are better prepared to grasp such fundamental religious concepts as the fatherhood of God, spiritual childhood, fraternity, unity, mercy, and hospitality. If we live in a home where there is space made for conversation and where we learn to listen to one another, we can understand that prayer is not a listing of demands, but a personal conversation with One who is deeply interested in what we have to say. If we live in homes that gather us together, then our children will be with us to witness how we respond to joyful news with gratitude to God, and to sad news with serenity, secure in his providential care. Gathered around the dinner table, our children will hear stories of the past sacrifices, successes, and failures of their forebears. Working next to us, they will witness our perseverance, patience, cheerfulness, and self-control. They will witness all of this naturally in the ordinary life of the home, and all of this will prepare them well to learn about morality in their ethics class and about sanctity in the stories of the saints.

In a thoughtful home, contact with God can be encouraged and respected, for there is time, space, and opportunity for this to happen. There is a place for family prayers, when a mother lights the Sabbath candles, or a father leads the family Rosary. There is opportunity to share the experience of praying to our guardian angel for an elusive parking place, and of praying for Grandma to get well and hearing that she is starting to improve. Perhaps most important, in the thoughtful home we can live with the daily experience of personal prayer as a heart-to-heart conversation with God. When children grow up around such prayer, learning to play quietly because Mommy is praying, they come to know—far more deeply than can be conveyed with words—that prayer is an ordinary daily activity, like working and playing and eating dinner.

Whether in ancient Rome or in my quiet Minnesota neighborhood, there is a place for God in our homes. In our homes we spend time with God, pay attention to him, get to know him, and learn to serve him. Like all our loved ones, for whom we make and keep our homes, we long for God to dwell in our thoughtful homes.

PART IV

Conclusion

Chapter 15
The Home and
the World

We who aspire to be thoughtful homemakers know what we are doing and why. We make our homes so that those who dwell there can flourish as human beings. This clarity of purpose gives clarity to our priorities, our plans, and even our to-do lists. We know where we are going, and therefore we can determine with confidence the best way to get there. We know that, although times and cultures change, human nature endures. This gives us reason to take counsel from our forebears, reconsidering their time-honored methods thoughtfully, adopting them when advisable, and adapting them to the particular circumstances of those entrusted to our care. We find help and support from those who share this profession, who share with us the desire and the work of making a thoughtful home. We find satisfaction and inspiration in the nobility of our goal and the creativity and intelligence required for our work. In our homes, thoughtfully and lovingly made, we can be at peace.

Our homes, however, have windows and doors. What happens when we look outside? What do we do with the anxiety that washes in when we open our front door and see a world that is a mess? As much as we love this family and this home, we are not blind to the suffering of those who do not dwell within our walls, who cannot benefit from the culture we are building within our homes. We want to use our gifts generously and wisely. We might reasonably wonder whether dedicating ourselves to making a thoughtful home is a self-indulgent choice.

It is certainly true that the world is a dreadful mess. All things considered, it is probably no more of a mess than at other times in human history, but it is also no less of a mess. And that is not reassuring. Yet the work of the home is messy work, and we homemakers have a lot of experience dealing with messes. As we stand at our front door and behold the mess of the world, we homemakers can respond in one of three ways.

The first is to believe that the only way to clean up the mess of our world is to do something big: to run for political office, to become a Hollywood producer, to found a religious order, to set up a non-profit. If we believe that only an organization with national or global reach can make a significant difference in the battle for culture, then we are likely to think that the home is unimportant by comparison. Like Mrs. Jellyby, we would see devotion to the home as something frivolous and self-indulgent, or at best something to be nobly sacrificed for the greater good. Responding to the world's mess in this way leads us to abandon our homes for the sake of trying to do something big enough to make a difference.

Doing great things in the world is a noble aspiration, and in every era, some are called to give up having a family and making a home in order to dedicate themselves to such noble endeavors. It might be possible for a few, equipped with extraordinary resources such as a willing spouse, intense self-knowledge, and a spine of steel, to accomplish historically important things while at the same time making and keeping a truly thoughtful home. For most of us, however, this is simply not realistic.

A second response to the mess of the world seems both more possible and less demanding. It is therefore more appealing to many of us. We accept that, absent the talents and energy of Joan of Arc or Harriet Beecher Stowe, it is impossible for us to save the world. Because we can't clean up the mess out there, we see our task as building up and fortifying the walls of our homes to shield our families and ourselves from the dirt and dangers that are pressing in.

This effort, as many have found to their great chagrin, is also unrealistic. We find, sooner or later, that it is simply not possible to keep the culture out. This is not because of cracks in our walls but because of the nature of those who live within them. Those who dwell in our homes are also made to live in our world. Our families are composed of human beings who crave culture and want to contribute to culture. No matter how hard we work, we cannot help but sense the looming failure of our efforts to keep the world out. We counter this with distraction, escaping our anxieties momentarily by checking our notifications, listening to a podcast, or placing an online order.

Happily, for thoughtful homemakers, there is a third response. This response is realistic, because thoughtful homemakers are familiar with reality. Professionally accustomed to messes of all sorts, we respond to the mess of the world by facing it squarely. We neither sacrifice our homes nor turn them into fortresses. Instead, we devote ourselves to cleaning up the messes of the world precisely by means of our wholehearted effort to make and keep a thoughtful home.

Our homes, because they are private and personal and made by us, are something that we always have the power to change. We can make them and strengthen them for the purpose of dealing with the timeless and inevitable problems of the human condition. We can also change them and adapt them in order to meet new challenges and deal with unforeseen problems. If smartphones threaten to destroy us, we can regulate their use within our homes or exclude them altogether. If gender ideology threatens to destroy us, we can make our homes places where girls and boys are allowed to be who and what they were created to be. If an undue emphasis on efficiency and productivity is the enemy, we can make our homes places where human bonds are valued over outcomes. If isolation and individualization are the problems, we can make our homes places where sharing and taking turns is promoted and privileged.

We homemakers have the power to make our homes centers of human flourishing in an increasingly inhumane world. We have the power to make them places where, simply by crossing the threshold, one is immersed in reality, bathed in human connection, and reminded of the presence of God. Each of us has the capacity to pay closer attention and to listen more carefully. We can seek help, learn new skills, and adopt better strategies. We can make our homes more attractive, more hospitable, more lifegiving. We can work more intensely and think more deeply; we can "harder hope and dearer love."[7] By doing all this, we help the members of our families, and anyone who enjoys our hospitality, to flourish as happy and virtuous human beings. By doing all this, we help them to become the sort of human beings who improve the world simply by being in it.

By means of our thoughtful homes and in the familiar details of our ordinary lives, we change the culture, making it better, making it healthier and more humane. We change not only the culture within our homes, but the wider culture in which our homes are made. For out of our thoughtful homes, in which people are attended to and cared for, come people who have been formed by those homes. Out of our thoughtful homes and into the mess of the world will come people who have acquired the habit of noticing others, and who have the generosity and serenity to listen to others, who have the confidence and spirit of initiative to care for others. A psychiatrist once told me that ninety percent of his patients didn't actually need his professional help, that what they needed was one really good friend. Our

7. Gerard Manley Hopkins, "Godhead Here in Hiding," translation of St. Thomas Aquinas' "Adoro Te Devote."

thoughtful homes form people who value friendship and are willing and able to be that really good friend. Thoughtful homes benefit not only our own families, but everyone they touch out in the world: their friends, their coworkers, their clients and patients and students, and even the person sitting next to them on the bus. Those who are listened to and cared for by us will be inclined to listen to and care for others. We homemakers help to sort out the mess of the world by filling it with individuals who have been made more human by means of our thoughtful homes.

Everything human is made, maintained, improved, or damaged by human beings who were formed, or deformed, in a home. Our children's school is staffed by teachers, principals, cafeteria workers, and custodians who were raised in homes. The McDonald's down the street is owned, managed, and staffed by individuals who were raised in homes. The drivers on our roads were raised in homes. Our police officers and firefighters and politicians were raised in homes. If the homes they came from were strong and healthy and good, and if the homes they now dwell in are strong and healthy and good, then all those individuals, our fellow citizens on whom we depend, will be better human beings. And that means that those institutions—our schools, businesses, and government—will be better. Our communities will be better. Our culture will be better. Our homes matter. They could not matter more.

We homemakers do not think of ourselves as leaders. This might be because our charges are so often stubborn, unruly, and full of attitude. In other words, they are normal human beings. They do not do what we want them to do, what we politely ask them to do, what we nag them to do. But true leadership is less about authority and obedience and more about influence. Every mother has been amused or unsettled by her toddler holding something vaguely rectangular to his ear and mimicking her phone call with embarrassing accuracy. We influence those who dwell in our homes by what we say and how we react, by our moods, our attitudes, and our priorities, by the print we choose for their bedroom wall and the cake we serve on their birthday. Even when we do have actual authority and obedient children, we are far more influential when others follow our lead in freedom, rather than by compulsion.

We question the lasting power of our influence, especially once our children begin to open the door (or gaze at a screen) and encounter the world beyond our walls. Certainly Hollywood, politicians, entrepreneurs, and celebrities have tremendous influence on the culture, and their influence can make us feel insignificant and helpless. Yet, our direct and personal influence upon our family and friends is more powerful than theirs. When, with our family on a Friday night, we watch a movie made by the most powerful producer in Hollywood and starring the most glamorous celebrities, we may not feel powerful or influential. And yet, by pointing out to our children how our emotions are being manipulated, or wondering aloud whether a plot line is plausible, we are more powerful than Hollywood. When we establish our dinner table as a smartphone free-zone, we are more powerful than Silicon Valley, not just with our families but with our dinner guests and our children's friends. This is not because we have kept out the culture by means of fortress walls. It is because we have used our influence to correct and purify what is harmful in the culture and elevate and honor that in it which is good.

The power of our influence is vastly multiplied by means of our thoughtful homes, for in them and by means of them we exert our influence all day and every day, even when we who make the home are not physically present there. We do this by making our homes places where people become accustomed to paying attention, thinking, listening, and caring. We do this by making them places that allow time and opportunity for shared experiences and for conversation about what has been shared. By making our homes places where our families want to be, and by being generous in the time we spend in those homes and in the thought we put into designing those homes, our family members are constantly influenced by us and by each other. This influence will prove to be deeper and more enduring than the influence of any cultural trend or zeitgeist.

Our homes matter. They have an unparalleled impact on us and on our families, and they can have a great impact on our friends and on those to whom we offer our hospitality. Our homes can isolate us or they can gather us together. Our homes can form us always to choose comfort or they can form us to value human bonds over such pleasures. Our homes can distract us from God or they can lead us to him.

Our culture does not give homemaking and the home a high value. Even we thoughtful homemakers give such things as housework and meal preparation a low priority when making our plans. Even we thoughtful homemakers struggle to "waste time" listening attentively to our husband or child without glancing at our phone. In matters of the home, we have not always been generous and wise with our time, our attention, and our resources.

Perhaps our failures have already had unfortunate consequences. Yet it is a luxury to indulge in regret or despair. We must count instead on the fact that we can always change, and that we can always change for the better. We may not yet feel capable of achieving the ideals put forth in this book, but we know that even now we are capable of putting away our phone for a little while, clearing the clutter off our dining room table, or setting a bowl of fresh fruit on our kitchen counter. Little by little, one choice at a time, we will start to notice that our homes are becoming thoughtful homes.

The thoughtful home will not be achieved without hard work, sacrifice, and a willingness to push back against an individualistic and consumer-oriented culture. Yet, we who choose to undertake this project can hope for rich rewards. When we embrace wholeheartedly the work of caring for those we love "just because they're there," we help to form whole and happy people capable of living a richly human life. Consequently, we will find ourselves living among such people. We will find ourselves sharing our homes and our lives with people who know how to give us the attention and care and love that we also need. We will be happy to look up from our work and find ourselves living in thoughtful homes.